Madina to Jerusalem

Encounters with the Byzantine Empire

ISMAIL ADAM PATEL

THE ISLAMIC FOUNDATION

Published by
THE ISLAMIC FOUNDATION,
Markfield Conference Centre,
Ratby Lane, Markfield, Leicester LE67 9SY, UK
Tel: (01530) 244944, Fax: (01530) 244946
E-mail: info@islamic-foundation.org.uk
Website: www.islamic-foundation.org.uk

Quran House, PO Box 30611, Nairobi, Kenya

PMB 3193, Kano, Nigeria

British Library Cataloguing in Publication Data
Patel, Ismail Adam
From Madina to Jerusalem: encounters with the Byzantine Empire
1. Yarmuk River, Battle of the, Syria, 636
2. Islamic Empire - Foreign relations - Byzantine Empire
3. Byzantine Empire - Foreign relations - Islamic Empire
4. Byzantine Empire - Foreign relations - 527–1081
I. Title
939.4'3

ISBN 0 86037 393 2

Typeset by: N.A. Qaddoura
Cover design: Nasir Cadir

Printed and bound in Great Britain by
Antony Rowe Ltd, Chippenham, Wiltshire

بسم الله الرحمن الرحيم

Contents

Transliteration Table

Consonants. Arabic

initial: unexpressed medial and final:

ء	’	د	d	ض	ḍ	ك	k
ب	b	ذ	dh	ط	ṭ	ل	l
ت	t	ر	r	ظ	ẓ	م	m
ث	th	ز	z	ع	‘	ن	n
ج	j	س	s	غ	gh	هـ	h
ح	ḥ	ش	sh	ف	f	و	w
خ	kh	ص	ṣ	ق	q	ي	y

Vowels, diphthongs, etc.

Short:	ـَ	a	ـِ	i	ـُ	u
long:	ـَا	ā	ـِي	ī	ـُو	ū
diphthongs:			ـَوْ	aw		
			ـَيْ	ay		

Introduction

History amongst other things allows us to judge a people's lineage and character. It further acts as a tool to justify actions and give weight to heritage. To others history is a means by which they may prepare for the future with a better understanding of the great heritage upon which their foundation is based. To those wishing to undermine Islam, the Islamic expansion into al-Sham (Syria, Palestine, Jordan and Lebanon) is used to consolidate Islamophobic views.

This book attempts not only to recount the military battles that led to the Muslims liberating al-Sham (area comprised of modern-day Lebanon, Syria, Jordan and Palestine) from the Byzantines but also to understand the reasons why the Byzantine confederates of al-Sham abandoned their former masters for Islam. It charts the course of Muslim presence from 8-15 AH/629-637 CE.

The first chapter traces the careers of the last three Byzantine emperors prior to Islam and the relationship of their subjects in al-Sham to the empire. This reveals the divisions within the empire on the basis of ethnic origin, religious beliefs and economic status.

The second chapter shows Islam's encounter with the Byzantine Empire from the time the Prophet Muhammad ﷺ

sent an invitation to Heraclius to accept Islam up to the accession of Abū Bakr ﷺ, the first Caliph.

The third chapter explores the battles between the Byzantine Empire and Islam, up to the liberation of Jerusalem.

The fourth chapter discusses the reasons for the Muslims' success in the hope of enabling those living in large multicultural societies to gain a more balanced and objective understanding of this period of Muslim history.

This project, which I began seven years ago in 1997, has come to fruition after the encouragement, assistance and prayers of many. All praise is to my Creator, whose Bounties and Mercies I cannot begin to enumerate even if *'all the World's water were provided as ink for me and wood as scribe to praise His Glory'*.

I am particularly grateful to Dr Daud Abdullah, David Middleton, Ishaq Dadhiwala, Naiem Qaddoura and my family who have patiently borne the burden of my absence. There have been many others who have encouraged me and to all I am grateful.

Leicester **Ismail Adam Patel**
Dhū al-Ḥijja 1425
January 2005

1

The Byzantine and Persian Empires Before Islam

Prior to the advent of Islam, at the beginning of the seventh century, two superpowers dominated the territories adjacent to the west and east of the Arabian Peninsula. The east was ruled by the great Persian Empire, extending from the borders of modern India to the upper Euphrates. The west was ruled by the great Roman Empire (see Map 1), from the shores of the Black Sea in the north to the Mediterranean in the south, including northern Africa, and from Britannia in the west to Syria and Arabia Petraea in the east. To the south of the Euphrates lay the largely barren desert land of the Arabian Peninsula, occupied by unruly Arabian nomads, which was of no direct strategic interest or economic value to either empires.

By 300, the Roman Empire had become so vast that Constantine, the Roman Emperor, partitioned it into two zones. By 363 the empire had acquired two capitals. Rome became the capital of the Western Empire and Constantinople, originally known as Byzantium, of the Eastern Empire.

Initially laws passed in either zone were automatically enforced throughout the whole empire, and the two capitals co-ordinated in all matters of state.[1] However, by 476 the

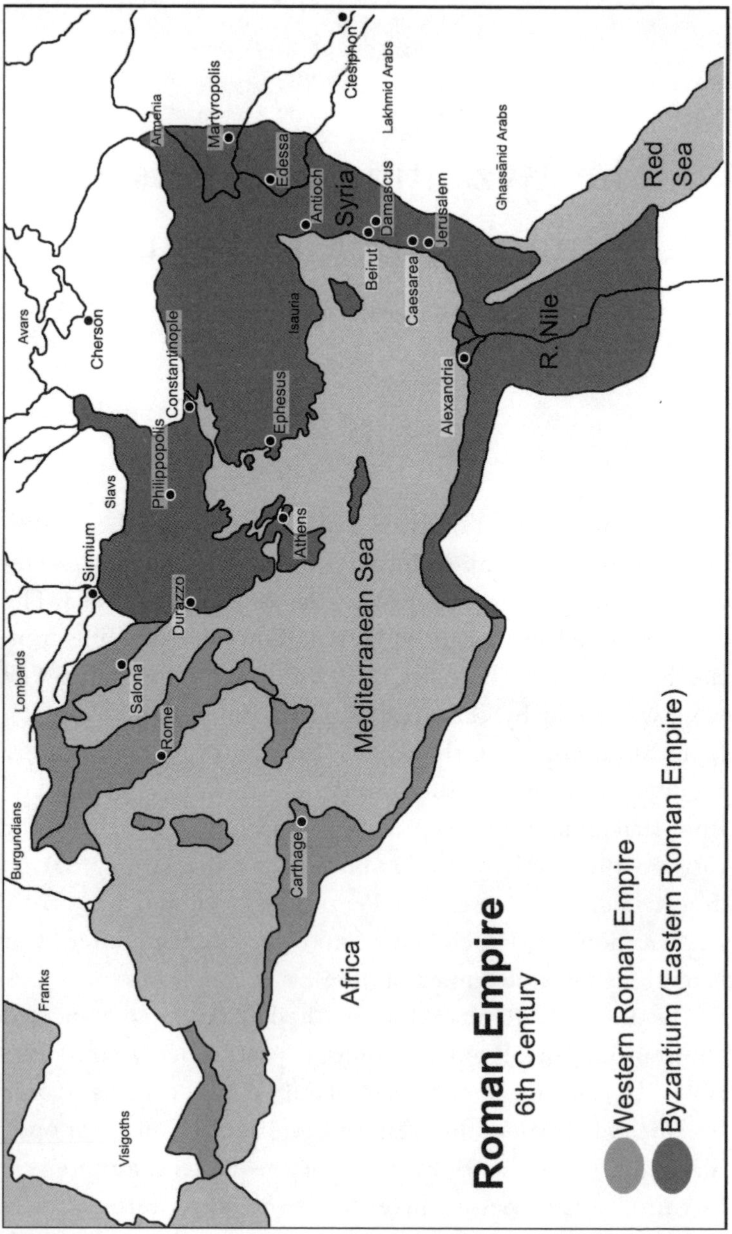

Map 1: Roman Empire

Western Empire was weakened by invasions and divisions while the Eastern Empire remained intact with all the splendour and heritage of the 'Greater Roman Empire'. Muslims therefore, encountered the Roman Empire with its capital in Constantinople, known in literature as the Byzantine Empire. Most Western scholars referring to the early Islamic encounters with Emperor Heraclius refer to it as a conflict with the Byzantine Empire; Muslim historians and scholars have generally preferred the term 'Roman Empire'. The Muslims have employed this term as the Qur'ān refers to the rulers of al-Sham as '*Rūm*', Romans. Further, it should be noted that Heraclius was crowned as the Roman Emperor.

From the fourth to the early seventh century the Byzantine Empire witnessed a succession of Emperors crowned and deposed at the vehement ambitions of military factions. From the end of Constantine's reign in 337 to the beginning of Heraclius' reign in 610 the Byzantine Empire witnessed a total of 22 Emperors. The citizens' fortunes changed depending on the Emperor's origin, religious belief and political hue. The position of the Christian churches on the doctrine of the Trinity, was settled in 325 at the first Council of Nicaea convened by Constantine I attended by 318 of the 1,800 bishops in the Roman Empire. God was defined as being three persons in one Godhead: God the Father, God the Son and God the Holy Ghost or Holy Spirit, in modern-day terminology. Already by the fifth century this doctrine of trinity was in disarray and provoked the religious strife which was to become the underlying cause of oppression of the Monophysites.

The Monophysites attempted to clarify and declare a stance on the God-man nature of Jesus Christ. The Mono (one) physites (nature) held the view that Christ had within him both divine and human natures fused into one, whereas

Nestorius, Patriarch of Constantinople and Antioch, stressed the human nature of Christ. This caused a great rift between the Orthodox and Monophysite Christians. The Monophysite doctrine was upheld by the Armenian Church in Anatolia, by most Egyptian Christians and the majority of the inhabitants of al-Sham (Syria, Palestine, Jordan and Lebanon).[2]

The instability within the empire caused by the religious split should not be underestimated. Apart from having a different belief, the Monophysites saw themselves as defenders of their tradition and status against the Graeco-Roman leaders in Constantinople and Rome, who were openly hostile to Monophysite teachings. In 608, a council was held in Constantinople in a final bid to unite the different factions of Christians within the empire. They came up with the compromise that Christ had two wills and energies existing side by side without mingling. In the event, the compromise failed to impress either group and the divisions persisted.

From 532, after Justinian had signed a peace treaty with Persia, up until 580 no major conflict of significance took place between the two 'superpowers'. In February-March 579 Chosroes I (531-579), the Persian leader died and his son Hormuzd became the new king. However, Hormuzd executed or blinded his brothers to ward off any challenge to his position and this brought dissension and tension within the Persian Empire. Aware of this dissension, Mundhir with Maurice, in late 580 attacked the Persians with the hope of occupying Ctesiphon, the capital of the Persian Empire. Unfortunately for Byzantine the expedition failed with Maurice and Mundhir becoming rivals.

It appears this Byzantine expedition did not deter Chosroes II (Parviz the Great) from seeking assistance in al-Sham after the Persian army deposed him in 590. Emperor Maurice and Patriarch Gregory of Antioch not only welcomed him but also provided the support of the Byzantine army to restore him to power. Maurice expelled Vahram VI, the rebel leader and reinstated Parviz as the King of Persia. The concession Maurice gained in return was a re-adjustment of frontiers in favour of Byzantium. The two 'superpowers' remained allies and in peaceful co-existence until the end of Maurice's reign.

PHOCAS

In 602, Emperor Maurice, after having halved the wages of the soldiers, made a second unwise decision. He ordered the army fighting the Avars to remain on the far side of the river Danube, in the winter cold. The army mutinied, proclaimed Phocas, a despot, as their leader, and marched on Constantinople. Maurice fled, only to be captured by Phocas along with his five sons and numerous allies. All were later executed and, for several days the heads of Maurice and his sons were put on show in the Camp of the Tribunal for the inhabitants of the city to view. Phocas claimed the title, power and authority of emperor.

The Persian King, Chosroes, noticing Phocas' treachery, attacked the Byzantine territory on the pretext of avenging his murdered friend, Maurice, who had earlier assisted him. The inadequacy of Phocas and his armies, coupled with the alliances that Chosroes had cultivated with the Jews and minority sects enabled him to occupy Armenia in 610 (which was lost to Byzantium in 591) and Asia Minor in 611. In late 611 he captured Antioch and by 614 he had conquered Jerusalem. It is alleged that 90,000 people were killed in the Holy City of Jerusalem. The Jews played a pivotal role, in some cases buying Christians from the Persians in order to kill them.

Theophanes, the Roman historian, records the events: 'in this year the Persians took Jordan, Palestine and its holy city in battle. At the hands of the Jews they killed many people in it. Some say 90,000.[3] The Jews, according to their means, bought the Christians and then killed them. The Persians captured and carted off to Persia Zacharia, the Patriarch of Jerusalem, the precious life-giving wood (supposed fragment of the True Cross on which Christ was crucified) and many prisoners (September 1, 614 – August 31, 615)'.[4] By the end of 616 the Persians had also overrun Egypt.

HERACLIUS

Phocas' incompetence in checking the Persians and the brutally oppressive regime he imposed on his subjects within the Byzantine Empire led to his overthrow by Heraclius. Heraclius sailed from Egypt in 610 with an icon of the Virgin Mary depicted on the mast of his ship. When Heraclius became emperor, the empire still stretched from the Euphrates to Gibraltar. An astute ruler, Heraclius promptly undertook several measures to settle internal divisions, in particular the religious rift. Heraclius engineered a religious compromise and declared that Christ had, indeed, two natures but only one will and one energy. The initial response from both the Monophysites and the Orthodox Christians was favourable, and the Bishops of Antioch, Akephaloi (in Cyprus) and Armenia, accepted the compromise formula. However, the religious leaders in Jerusalem and surrounding Palestine, Sinai and the Bishop of the Nile, Arsinoe, rejected the compromise, with the consequence of festering dissent, notably in the area of al-Sham.

By and large, the initial impact of Heraclius' effort was modestly successful in healing the religious rift. His second task was to check the foreign threat, especially that of Persian advances. He introduced martial law, began re-organizing his army and, simultaneously, sued for peace with the Persians. The only reply he obtained from the Persian king was: 'I shall not spare you until you have renounced the crucified one whom you call God and bow before the sun.'[5]

Diplomacy exhausted, Heraclius turned his administrative skills to restructuring and restoring the fragmented Byzantine army. After twelve years, in 622, the day after Easter, he sailed out of Constantinople with a huge conscript force. The ensuing conflict and its outcome ensured that Heraclius entered into the realms of Western historical legend. Before this decisive conflict, its outcome was revealed to the Prophet Muḥammad ﷺ in Makka through a verse in the Qur'ān.[6]

The clash of the giants took place amid great religious passion and fervour. The Byzantine forces surged forward steadily and systematically, destroying the Persians as they advanced. As they advanced, the army razed houses and farms, often whole villages to the ground, and slew the Persians they captured. They plundered the corpses, taking corslets, helmets and other arms. Looting its way, the Byzantine army amassed to inflict the final blow in 627, which pierced the very heart of the Persian Empire.

The last days of the battles are recorded by Theophanes:

> Goundabousan one of the commanders of a thousand of Sarbaros' army went over to Mezezios along with five other men. Three were Counts, the other two Officers. Mezezios brought them to the Emperor. He said, 'When Chosroes fled from Dastagerd to Ctesiphon he contracted dysentery and wanted to crown his son Merdasa who was his child by Seirem. He left his first-born son Siroes (Kavad II) and his brothers and wives behind. When Siroes learned that Chosroes wanted to crown Merdasa, he was dismayed and sent a man to me, saying, "Come across the river so I can meet you." I was afraid to cross because of Chosroes and told Siroes to write. Siroes wrote, "You know the wicked Chosroes has destroyed the Persian state.

He wants to crown Merdasa and has contempt for me, his first-born. If you speak to the army and make it accept me, I promise to increase the wages and make peace with the Byzantine Emperor; we will live well. Hurry with your army so I can become king. I promise to unite and exalt you all, especially yourself.' Through his close friend I told him that I would talk to the army and work on it. On March 23 we intend to march on Chosroes. He sent me to you, my lord, because he respects the Byzantine Empire, which once saved Chosroes.' Heraclius sent a messenger back to Siroes, telling him to release all Roman prisoners, arm them and move against Chosroes. Siroes obeyed the Emperor. Chosroes was captured and they put heavy irons on his feet and neck, then put him in the *house of darkness*, which he himself had fortified in order to store his money there. They gave him poor bread and water and starved him, for Siroes said, 'Let him eat the gold which he accumulated in vain for which he starved many and devastated the world.' He sent every one of Chosroes' enemies to curse him, beat him and spit on him. After five days of these, Siroes ordered him, his son Merdasa (whom he had wished to crown) and all the rest of his sons killed. Thus, in these terrible conditions, Chosroes gave up his wicked life.

Then Siroes wrote to Heraclius sending him good news of bloody Chosroes' end. He made a permanent peace with the Emperor and restored to him all the imprisoned Christians, the captives from all over Persia (including the patriarch Zacharia) and the precious life-giving wood which Persians took from Jerusalem.

With Chosroes dead and Siroes (Kavad II) an ally at the helm in Persia, Heraclius returned to Constantinople in triumph and majesty. With great pomp he had returned a fragment of the 'true cross' to Jerusalem. Placed thus at the very pinnacle of the only 'superpower', Heraclius might have pondered over his and his empire's great fortune and the establishment of the greatest power in the world. The year 2/622 signalled a particular turning point of fortune in his favour. But in the same year of the second *hijrī*, his contemporaries could not have concerned themselves about a small battle between Muḥammad ﷺ and some of his own clansmen in the barren Arabian desert valley of Badr. Yet, of the war between the mighty empires, only broken statues and weather-beaten coliseums, built with the sweat and blood of slaves remain. In contrast, the victory registered by just over three hundred men in Badr,[7] determined that the *takbīr* (*Allāh Akbar*) is today heard in almost every corner of the world.

Heraclius in Jerusalem was at the zenith of his glory and power and his empire at its most secure. From the position he had won he must have felt unassailable: he had just defeated the Persians and secured former Roman borders; internally, the wrangling within the church was muted. There appeared to be no threat to the empire. He was able to boast a first-hand knowledge of his vast dominion, including the terrain in al-Sham, Mesopotamia and Armenia. He was not only an emperor but also a first-rate battle-hardened commander of the armies and navy. He inspired terror and awe in his enemies and no one dared oppose him. As emperor, commander and captain, he was in absolute command of the empire, well able to meet any challenge that might arise.

AL-SHAM

Until the death of the emperor Maurice in 602, the Byzantium Empire as a whole functioned splendidly and in relative peace for its subjects. However, the eight years of Phocas' rule were a period of considerable disorder and suffering in the empire, especially its Balkan territories. The darkest shadow of oppression in the history of Byzantium was cast by their brutalities of this period. In al-Sham, instability was greatly aggravated after the Persian attack. The Persian occupation lasted just under a decade, as the Persians did not occupy Antioch until 613, Jerusalem in 614, and Egypt by the end of 616.

Although Phocas was widely despised, his subjects' contempt for the Persians was even greater. Many inhabitants hoped for a return of the Byzantine masters to save them from the savage cruelty of the Persians. Historians record that the army used to defeat the Persians was partly made up from the Arabs of al-Sham, the Ghassānids, and that the alliance between these Arabs and the Byzantines was still strong and cohesive. After approximately ten years of persecution at the hands of the Persians, Byzantine rule returned once again. For some 'brothers in religion' this was a welcome return to the *status quo ante.*

Most Western historians have assumed that the decay that befell Christianity also caused a decline in the empire. However, the Christian decay did not have any political repercussions. Evidence of the cohesion of the empire lies in the fact that because of the empire, Christianity was able to spread from its base in Rome to all the Mediterranean countries, Abyssinia and up the shores of the Red Sea. The same political cohesion enabled Christianity to move from al-Sham to the adjoining Ghassānid tribes and the populous banks of the Euphrates.[8]

Prior to the Muslims' liberation of al-Sham from Byzantine rule, the majority of its inhabitants resided within city walls. All the major cities, including Damascus, Antioch, Aleppo, Caesarea and Jerusalem were fortified with walls, their exits and entrances controlled by guarded gates. The government officers, merchants and landowners who used to venture outside the walls to visit their fields and pastures returned by dusk to the safety provided by the fortified walls. The poor who worked in the city as well as peasants, farmers and shepherds who worked outside had to leave the cities before dusk. The open areas were not safe from bandits who emerged at night to pillage the open fields. Thus the empire could properly protect only those of its subjects permitted to reside within the fortified towns.

To appreciate the day-to-day life of the people under the Byzantine Empire, a brief account of two major cities follows. This will serve to give some sense of the economic, military, theological and civil order and indicate the status of the masses in relation to their Byzantine masters.

Antioch

Antioch was one of the foremost cities in the Byzantine Empire, enjoying a special position equal to Alexandria, Constantinople and even Rome. At the peak of its glory around 165 the city had a population of over six hundred thousand.[9] Between 386 and 393 there were one hundred thousand Christians resident in Antioch. Surrounded by fertile land that yielded good quality produce – olives, as well as wheat and barley, and garden vegetables, the region's cucumber being particularly famous.[10]

During the reign of Emperor Maurice the Byzantine troops in al-Sham mutinied. The soldiers had wanted Germanicus to lead them but the Emperor had appointed Philippicus. The mutiny that started in April 588 continued until 589. It came to an end only after the intervention of Patriarch Gregory of Antioch. Highly respected by the troops, he delivered a politically moving speech, steered the soldiers into accepting Philippicus and promised them full pardon.

The animosity between the Christian Roman rulers and the Jews surfaced in 592/93 when a Jewish resident of Antioch committed a sacrilege for which the entire Jewish community was punished. The Jews had the centre part of their heads shaved and were expelled from the city.[11]

The lifestyle of villagers outside the city walls was in sharp contrast to that of the affluent city dwellers. They only came into the city occasionally to sell their produce and being peasants, they were shunned. The language barrier, deliberately maintained by the Greek-speaking upper classes against the Syriac-speaking peasants, accentuated the divide and prevented intermingling of the social classes. A fixed tax, the amount being irrespective of the harvest, was levied on the peasants. It was also not uncommon for landlords to charge a fifty per cent interest rate on loans of wheat made to peasants before the harvest, to be paid after it. It can be concluded that peasants working for landlords were registered for purposes of taxation under the estates of their landlords, and were not allowed to leave the estates under which they registered. Their condition was close to slavery.[12]

During the reign of Maurice, Antioch received a financial boost from the Persian Emperor Chosroes who sent many gifts, money and a cross, ornamented with gold and precious stones to the Patriarch Gregory. This was in return for the Emperor and Gregory playing a leading role in restoring him to the Persian throne.

The murder of Maurice brought the vicious Phocas (602-610) to power, which weakened the empire in all respects. The mainly Monophysite Christians of Antioch suffered severe persecution at the hands of Phocas. The inhabitants of the city and the physical structure suffered further when the Persians raided Antioch first in 606 then, for a second time, in 607 before finally capturing and occupying it in 611. They carried away with them many prisoners, looted gold from the churches and robbed the city of almost all its valuable items. The Persian invasion of Antioch resulted in the collapse of the city's infrastructure. Theophanes in his *Chronicles* reports that the Persians forced all the Christians to become Nestorians. The success rate of this campaign has not been documented.

Heraclius was not able to expel the Persians from Antioch until 628 when the Roman captives were released from Persia.

After the initial expulsion of the Jews in 592/93, they seemed to have returned to Antioch, apparently under the protection of the Persians during their raids of 606 and 607. However, peace did not last for long, for riots broke out in September 610. These disturbances erupted after the Jews had murdered Patriarch Anastasius, mutilated his body, dragged it along the main streets and then burned it, along with many others. Phocas despatched a substantial force to punish and crush the Jews, and restore order. A range of stiff fines were imposed upon the Jews.[13]

From 628 onwards, Heraclius worked towards rebuilding Antioch. He made al-Sham his headquarters and the seat of his power. In the fifty years prior to the emergence of Islam, the security and status of the inhabitants waxed and waned, depending upon the respect of their creed by their masters. The Jews on the other hand remained oppressed to varying degrees with their basic freedoms denied. The Monophysites suffered from the Orthodox masters of the empire. Under intermittent Persian occupation, the Jews enjoyed some measure of power and they took full advantage of this to settle old scores.

After the restoration of Byzantine rule in Antioch by Heraclius, the Christians took full revenge against the Jews, who had allied with the Persian enemy.

Jerusalem

The Roman Emperor Constantine's conversion to Christianity raised substantially the status and importance of Palestine, and of Jerusalem. Constantine was the first Roman Emperor to embrace Christianity and through him the revival of

Christianity within the empire and beyond was assured. Macarius, the Bishop of Jerusalem (at the time also called Aelia), brought to the attention of the newly converted Emperor in Constantinople, the poor state of the religiously significant sites of Christianity which were sanctified by Jesus in Jerusalem. Macarius managed to win the support of the Emperor's mother, Helena, who accepted his invitation to visit Jerusalem in 326.

According to Christian traditions, Helena, with the aid of Bishop Macarius, identified the site of Jesus' crucifixion, his burial place and the 'True Cross' on which he was believed to have been crucified. It was miraculously located beneath a former temple of Venus, which caught fire just at the time of Helena's visit. Also, in Helena's presence, while removing the foundations of the Capitoline temple,[14] workmen uncovered an empty tomb, which was then identified as that of Christ.

These discoveries aided Helena's decision to construct splendid Churches: The Sepulchre (Resurrection) at the site where the 'True Cross' was discovered, the Church of the Nativity at Bethlehem and the Church of Eleona.[15] Helena set the precedent for other rich Christians to erect shrines in Jerusalem. Gradually the city began to be engulfed in Christian shrines and to attain the status of the 'True City' in the eyes of the Christians.

With the coming of Christianity, the Jews were the first to suffer in Jerusalem. They were barred from entering the city except on one day of the year, the 9th of Av, (the date in the Jewish calendar, that coincides with the destruction of their Temple) when they were allowed to wail at the al-Buraq (Western or Wailing) Wall. The persecution did not stop at the Jews, but was extended also to the Samaritans and Monophysites, both considered heretics by the ruling masters.

With the city beginning to play a pivotal role in the faith of Christianity, the influx of Christian families from far and wide continued to swell the Christian population of Jerusalem. As pilgrims flocked in, churches and shrines were erected on every spot that had the remotest connection with Jesus or Mary. This influx from the far-flung corners of the empire demanded from the Christian authorities in Jerusalem the identification of more historically interesting and significant sites. As a consequence, many other sites were located: the House of Caiaphas, where part of Jesus' trial had taken place; the Garden of Gethsemane, the site where Jesus had prayed and been betrayed by Judas (Mark 14: 32–42); the Praetorium, the residence of Pontius Pilate, which in fact was located in the area of the Tower of David and not as pointed out to pilgrims in the Tyropoean Valley; the Sheep pool, the site of the Virgin Birth and the place of healing of paralytics; and the Pool of Siloam where Jesus sent the blind man to wash and be healed.[16]

The imperial policy of making Jerusalem a Christian city alienated all other faiths and tribes. The social, political and economic arrangements ensured that most people were either forced to embrace Christianity or abandon the city. Accordingly, by the end of the fourth century, most peasants living in the vicinity of Jerusalem had converted to Christianity. This alienating, oppressive policy played a role in the fall of Palestine to the Persians.

The Persian army approached Jerusalem in 614 and found many allies, in particular, the Jews, who not only welcomed them, in order to escape the oppression of the Christians, but also assisted them in the destruction of Churches and the slaying of Christians. As stated earlier, Jews, according to their means, bought the Christians and then killed them. A Christian monk, Antiochus Strategos, provides a contemporary account of the Persian capture of Jerusalem:

'...the evil foeman entered the city in great fury, like infuriated beasts and irritated serpents. They slew all whom they found. Like mad dogs they tore with their teeth the flesh of the faithful, and respected none at all, neither male nor female, neither young nor old, neither child nor baby, neither priest nor monk, neither virgin nor widow...They listened not to appeals of supplicants...On the contrary they destroyed persons of every age, massacred them like animals, cut them in pieces, mowed sundry of them down like cabbages, so that all alike had severally to drain the cup full of bitterness. Lamentation and terror might be seen in Jerusalem. Holy churches were burned with fire, others were demolished, majestic altars fell prone, sacred crosses were trampled underfoot, life-giving icons were spat upon by the unclean. Then their wrath fell upon priests and deacons: they slew them in their churches like dumb animals.

'Thereupon the Jews rejoiced exceedingly and they approached the edge of the reservoir and called to the children of God (Christians), while they were shut up therein, and said to them: "If you would escape from death, become Jews and deny Christ and then you shall step up from your place and join us. We will ransom you with our money, and you shall be benefited by us." But their plot and desire were not fulfilled. Because the Christians chose death for Christ's sake rather than to live godlessness. When the Jews saw the steadfast uprightness of the Christians, then they were agitated with lively ire, like evil beasts, and thereupon imagined another plot. ...They gave the Persians silver, and they bought a Christian and slew him like a sheep...When the people were carried into Persia, and the Jews were left in Jerusalem, they began with their own hands to demolish and burn such of the holy churches as were left standing.'[17]

The Patriarch Zacharia with 35,000 prisoners and the fragment of the 'True Cross' from the Church of the Sepulchre, were taken away as prisoners to Persia. As a gesture of good-will and a token of appreciation for assisting the Persians gain Jerusalem, the Jews were given administrative power in Jerusalem. This time, the Jews are alleged to have avenged their mistreatment by banishing Christians from the city. Whatever was not destroyed during the invasion of Jerusalem by the Persians, the Jews made sure they razed to the ground, even the Church of Resurrection was not spared.[18]

The Persians, after a period allowed the Christians to practise their faith. Under the leadership of Modestus, most of the Churches and Holy sites began to be renovated and the pace of renovation gained momentum after Heraclius' victory over the Persians in 627.

Heraclius, triumphant after his battle with the Persians, personally returned the fragment of the 'True Cross' to Jerusalem on 21 March 630. As he approached the city with an entourage of royal guards, dignitaries, monks, and bishops, crowds of Christians gathered outside the city gate to welcome him. The Emperor, robed in a purple gown with silk woven dragons, mounted upon a horse adorned with gold trappings, and holding high the Cross encased in a glittering golden case, made his entry. The path was lined with Byzantine soldiers in full armour, bearing the royal standard. Musicians and singers added to the grandiose spectacle. The pomp and ostentation disgusted the Patriarch of Jerusalem, who rebuked the Emperor[19] and recommended the observance of greater humility when entering a holy city.

However, beneath the smiles and applause there lurked for many uncertainty and fear. This, unfortunately, was realized more quickly than could have been anticipated, for the wheel of fortune turned once more against the Jews and Heraclius banished them from the Holy City. He ordered that they should not come within three miles of it.[20]

According to Butler, the adversity of exile from Jerusalem for the Jews was slight compared to the edict that followed instructing the provinces throughout the empire to persecute the Jews – 'something like a general massacre followed.' The Patriarch ordered the establishment of a week's fast every year. This fast in the first week of Lent with the Copts is called *The Fast of Heraclius*.

After Patriarch Zacharia's death in 630, Modestus became Patriarch of Jerusalem. His reign was short-lived, however. He died in 634, to be replaced by Sophronius who was later to accomplish the peace treaty with ʿUmar ibn al-Khaṭṭāb ﷺ, the second Caliph of Islam.

THE ARAB-BYZANTINE RELATIONSHIP

The most powerful and influential of the confederates of the Byzantium Empire in the al-Sham region before the coming of the Prophet Muḥammad ﷺ were the powerful tribe of Ghassānid. Arab-Roman relations began to be established from as early as 64 BC under the leadership of Pompey. The Ghassānids displaced the Salihids from the control of al-Sham and thereby became the main federate group in the early part of the sixth century. Following in the footsteps of Emperor Anastasius (491-518), the Ghassanids converted to the Monophysite creed of Christianity around 510. The Monophysite beliefs penetrated deep among these people. By the end of the sixth and the beginning of the seventh centuries the Ghassānid Arabs were securely allied to Byzantium and most embraced Christianity as Monophysites.[21] Their affiliation to Christianity was affirmed in the Heraclian victory bulletin over the Persians which refers to 'our Christ-loving state'.[22]

Prior to the rise of Islam, al-Ḥārith (Aretha) reigned as the supreme king of the Ghassānids. His son Mundhir succeeded him in 569. In 580 the Arab-Byzantine relationship reached its peak when, under the orders of Emperor Tiberius (578-582), Mundhir played a major role in the implementation of a religious policy designed to unite the different factions. Tiberius was impressed by his efforts and crowned Mundhir, elevating his status from chief of the Ghassānids to chief of the Byzantine subjects in his territory. Generous gifts flowed his way and a most harmonious relationship existed. The letter of Bishop Simeon of Beth Arsham, indicates the appreciation of Mundhir's efforts: 'We inform you, O beloved, that on (20 Jan 524) we left Hirta de Numan together with the priest Abraham, son of Euphrasius, who had been sent by Emperor Justin to Mundhir, King of the Arabs, to make peace, about which we already wrote in a previous letter. We and all the believers here are indebted to his favours, for he assisted our faction.'

After Mundhir returned from Emperor Tiberius in Constantinople with crown and glory, he and Maurice, *magister militum* at the time, jointly advanced against the territory of the Persians at Ctesiphon and their confederates, the Lakhmids. However, the Byzantines, having reached the environs of Ctesiphon, were forced to make a hasty retreat in the face of a counter-attack by the Persians. In the confusion, and to provide a scapegoat for the failure, Maurice accused Mundhir of treachery, in particular of having informed the Persians beforehand of the advance which led to the destruction of a bridge over the river Euphrates by the Persians.

Upon Mundhir's return home, he was informed through his intelligence sources that the Lakhmids, with the aid of the Persians, were planning to attack his quarters. Without delay, Mundhir advanced to check the offensive. He successfully defeated the Lakhmids and pillaged their camp at Ḥirā. The power of the Ghassānids and the empire's dependence on their military strength to control the borders and the population of al-Sham is self-evident. Mundhir, in his short career, campaigned five times against the Lakhmids, with success on all occasions.

Meanwhile, Maurice in a personal vendetta against Mundhir raised the charge of treachery at the court of the Emperor Tiberius. Maurice convinced the Emperor and a summons for Mundhir's arrest promptly followed. The decision to arrest Mundhir and take him to Constantinople sowed the seed of resentment in the Arab-Byzantine relationship.

To the great surprise of the Emperor, his hitherto steadfast and devoted Ghassanid subjects rose in rebellion after hearing of the arrest. In his absence, Mundhir's four sons, under the leadership of Nuʿmān, raised arms and attacked *Magnus Castra* (possibly Ḥirā), where they killed many and took much booty. They further attacked towns and districts in al-Sham, including Bostra, with remarkable success. The first Ghassanid rebellion shook the empire and the success of their forays underscored their power.

The Byzantine leadership despatched Magnus to deal with the problem. After amassing a huge army, Magnus installed Mundhir's brother as king. The latter died within a month and Magnus' plan was thwarted. Magnus tried to call upon Nuʿmān for a conference. The latter, however, suspected treachery and sent a substitute. Once again Magnus' plan failed and some days later he died.

The Emperor, Tiberius also died in the same year, 582. This ushered Maurice to the Byzantine throne, a Dyophysite with an immense hatred for the Monophysites and in particular of Mundhir,[23] whom he had earlier accused of treachery.

In the hope of reconciliation, Nuʿmān went in person to Constantinople to plead for his father. However, he was charged with treason and put in prison with his father. Thus began the darkest phase in Arab-Byzantine relations.

After the murder of Maurice, Phocas' reign initially saw the fortunes of the Ghassānids improve. Mundhir was released from prison and this was of great benefit to the empire. When the Persians under Chosroes II attacked Byzantine territories, it was the Ghassānids who were called upon to participate in protecting the borders and they did so with great gusto.[24]

Yet the harmony between the Ghassānids and the Emperor did not last long. Within a short time, the true colours of the brutal Dyophysite, Phocas, became manifest as the Monophysite Ghassānids bore the full brunt of his cruelties. Bonosus was placed as a commander of the army that in 609 ruthlessly quelled the Monophysite insurrection that had begun earlier in 608.

The Monophysites of al-Sham saw their fortunes evaporating by the day under the rule of Phocas. News of Heraclius' sailing from Egypt to eliminate the tyrant Phocas in 610 must have been eagerly awaited. It seems almost inevitable that the Ghassānids assisted Nicetas, Heraclius' cousin, if not with manpower then with intelligence and definitely in spirit. His confrontation and eventual defeat of Bonosus in 610 naturally delighted the Ghassānids.

The loyalty of the Ghassanids to the empire still remained unquestionable. This can be seen from the fact that they were in the forefront with Heraclius in fighting against the Persians. They had become an integral part of the empire and their future was invested in that of the empire.

Under Heraclius, the Ghassānids and Arab *foederati* breathed another sigh of relief. A new personality by the name of Jabala began to dominate the Ghassānid kingdom. The Ghassānids' participation against the Persians in the Heraclian era is well documented, and Heraclius must have relied upon their influence to implement his policy of religious compromise – *Monoenergism*. Shahid states: 'The dominant figure of Jabala in this decade also suggests that Heraclius may have returned to the Ghassānids the privileged position they had enjoyed during the reign of Justinian.'[25] Their role in the Battle of Yarmuk and in particular the appointment of Jabala as one of the commanders is a testimony of their close alliance with the empire and the empire's reliance upon them. A relationship that began in the era of Pompey had solidified into a durable bond that survived the disruptions it suffered. All the historical evidence suggests that a close and cohesive relationship between the Arabs and Byzantines developed during this period and that it could not be broken by external influence.

JEWISH-BYZANTINE RELATIONS

By contrast the relationship of the Byzantines with the Jews was very negative. The Byzantine-Christian authorities did not consider the Jews as allies. Heavy constraints were imposed upon them and they were subjected to harsh forms of oppression. It was one of the most forlorn periods in their bleak history, as the edicts show. It was decreed that a Jew could not testify against an Orthodox Christian though he could testify against another Jew.[26] Jews could neither serve in the army nor in the government. A law passed in 418 decreed, 'Those persons who live in the Jewish superstition shall hereafter be barred from seeking entrance to the imperial service...those persons who are bound to the perversity of this race and who are proved to have sought armed imperial services shall unquestionably be released from the cincture of office and they shall not be protected by the patronage of their earlier merits.'[27] After Emperor Constantine embraced Christianity, Jerusalem became inaccessible to the Jews. The exile from the Holy City illustrates the contempt and hostility meted out to the Jews throughout the empire. The Jewish community during this period were denied basic human rights comparable to others and were placed on a level with slaves.

NOTES

1. Whitting, Phillip, *Byzantium: an Introduction* (Oxford, 1971), p. 3.
2. Hourani, Albert, *A History of the Arab People* (London 1991), p. 8.
3. Sebeos the Armenian, states 57,000 slain and 35,000 taken captive.
4. Theophanes, *The Chronicles of Theophanes*. Trans. Harry Turtledove (Philadelphia, 1982), p. 11.
5. Whitting, Phillip, op. cit., p. 42.
6. *Sūra al-Rūm* 30: 1-3, '*Alif. Lām. Mīm.* The Romans have been defeated in a land close by, but they, (even) after (this) defeat of theirs, will soon be victorious...' This *sūra* was revealed in 615-616 in Makka (before the Prophet's ﷺ migration to Madina) when the Persians had the upper hand in the war and were in control of al-Sham. The non-believers at the time taunted the Prophet ﷺ because of the prediction in the Qur'ān.
7. This is the first major battle in the history of Muslims. The Makkan Quraysh had advanced in a well-equipped force of about one thousand men towards Madina, where the Prophet ﷺ had taken refuge, in order to attack and annihilate the Muslims. However, a company of 313 Muslims were able to defeat the Quraysh in the engagement at Badr.
8. Haykal, Muhammad Hussain, *The Life of Muhammad* (North American Trust Publ., 1976), p. 7.
9. Downey, Glenville, *A History of Antioch in al-Sham* (Princetown, 1961), p. 583.
10. Ibid., p. 21.
11. Downey, Glenville, op. cit., p. 571.
12. Liebeschuetz, J. H. W. G., *Antioch - City and Imperial Administration in the Later Byzantium Empire* (Oxford, Clarendon Press, 1972), p. 66.
13. Downey, Glenville, op. cit., p. 573.
14. *The Oxford Dictionary of Byzantium* (New York, 1991), p. 1034.
15. The original Church of Eleona was destroyed and on the spot now lies the Basilica of the Sacred Heart.
16. *The Oxford Dictionary of Byzantium*, op. cit., p. 1035.
17. Geanakoplos, Deno John, *Byzantium – Church, Society and Civilisation seen through contemporary eyes* (Chicago 1984), p. 266.
18. Avi-Yonah, Michael, *A History of the Holy Land* (London, 1969), p. 181.
19. Butler, Alfred J., *The Arab Conquest of Egypt (and the last thirty years of the Roman dominion)* (Oxford 1978), p. 131.
20. Theophanes, op. cit., p. 30.
21. Stratos, Andreas N., *Byzantium in the Seventh Century*, Vol. I, pp. 602-634. Trans. Marc Ogilvie Grant (Amsterdam, 1968), p. 19.
22. Shahid, Irfan, *Rome and The Arabs, A Prolegomenon to the study of Byzantium and the Arabs* (Washington, 1984), Vol. I, p. 944.

23. Under Tiberius, Mundhir was kept in Constantinople and enjoyed a degree of freedom worthy of his status. When Maurice became Emperor, Mundhir was summarily exiled. *The Seventh Century in West Syrian Chronicles*, Trans. Andrew Palmer (Liverpool, Liverpool University Press, 1993), p. 113.
24. Shahid, Irfan, op. cit., p. 622.
25. Ibid., p. 647.
26. Geanakoplos, Deno John, op. cit., p. 100.
27. Ibid., p. 266.

2

Encounters

FIRST PHASE

The Prophet Muḥammad ﷺ began his mission in Makka around 610. His call to Islam was rejected by many of his clansmen. Those who embraced Islam were harshly persecuted; eventually, the polytheists among the Quraysh planned to assassinate the Prophet ﷺ. Their plots failed as Allah commanded the Prophet to migrate to Madina in order to establish an Islamic Society. However, even in Madina the Muslims were not safe from the Makkan polytheists. The Muslims' victory at Badr in 2 (second year of *Hijra*) proved a turning point for the growing Muslim community.

Allah, through the Qur'ān, commanded His Messenger Muḥammad ﷺ to proclaim His message to the world:

> *O Messenger, proclaim the (Message) which has been sent to you from your Lord. And if you do not, you would not have conveyed His message. Allah will defend you from the people (who mean mischief). Surely Allah does not guide the people who reject faith.* (al-Mā'ida 5: 67)

> *...So proclaim openly what you are commanded, and turn away from the polytheists...* (al-Ḥijr 15: 94)

The Prophet ﷺ approached his Companions and commanded:

> Listen, O people, Allah has sent me as His Messenger and a Prophet of mercy for all the world. Mind that you do not fall into dissension like the disciples of Jesus. Go and convey the divine message from me.[1]

The truce signed at Ḥudaybiya between the Muslims and the Makkan polytheists in the year 6 AH, provided a respite from battle and battle preparations. The Prophet ﷺ began to send letters to the neighbouring chiefs, tribal leaders, kings and emperors to widen the call of Islam. In early 7/628 the Prophet ﷺ sent Ḥārith ibn 'Umar with a letter to the Governor of Buṣrā in al-Sham.

Ḥārith ibn 'Umar never reached Buṣrā. On his way, he was met at a place called Mu'ta by Shuraḥbīl ibn ʿAmr, a chieftain of the Ghassanid tribe, who became so infuriated with the content of the letter that he murdered the Prophet's messenger in cold blood. Even by ancient standards, this constituted a gross violation of acceptable practice. The news of Ḥārith's death was received with great sorrow in Madina.

During the same period, the Prophet ﷺ sent fifteen men for the purpose of teaching Islam to Dhāt al-Ṭalḥ north of Madina towards the outskirts of al-Sham. Here too the messengers were put to death in cold blood.

These murders led the Prophet ﷺ to rally his *Ṣaḥāba* (Companions) and march upon Mu'ta. This was a hazardous call as, at the time, Makka and other major Arabian cities were still hostile to Muslims and to challenge an external enemy at this juncture posed grave dangers. Further, Mu'ta was the centre for the manufacture of swords and as such heavily fortified and guarded by the Byzantine army. An attack on Mu'ta would require a large and well-equipped fighting force, which the Muslims lacked. However, the Prophet's ﷺ

love for his envoys was great, and their murders demanded retaliation. Thus, in early 8/629, three thousand *Ṣaḥāba* volunteered to avenge the deaths of their brothers in Islam. For this crucial expedition the Prophet ﷺ honoured Zayd ibn Ḥārith ؓ,[2] a close Companion with the command.

Zayd ؓ was the son of Ḥārith ؓ, a freed slave. '... Zayd was a fit commander and he was one of the dearest persons to me...'[3]

The appointment of Zayd ؓ, a freed slave, to such an honoured position, was a strong proof of the egalitarian temperament of Islam. Islam sought to rid society of prejudices based on lineage, race or status and the Qur'ān says:

> *...the most noble among you in the sight of Allah is (he who is) the most God-fearing.* (al-Ḥujurāt 49: 13)

Before the army's departure, the Prophet ﷺ informed his three thousand *Ṣaḥāba* that in the event of Zayd's martyrdom, Jaʿfar ibn Abī Ṭālib ؓ[4] was to assume command, and in the event of Jaʿfar's martyrdom, ʿAbdullāh ibn Rawāḥa ؓ[5] was to take his place. The Prophet ﷺ accompanied the army for some distance, bidding them farewell with the instruction not to kill any women, children, nor to destroy trees, houses or monasteries.[6] Among the force was a recent convert to Islam. This individual, Khālid ibn al-Walīd ؓ, was one of the greatest military geniuses of all time,[7] whose skills as a commander were decisive in the conquest of Iraq and al-Sham. [*see* Map 2]

The Ghassānids and the Byzantines soon received news of the advance of the Muslim force. Theophanes reports that the Quraysh from Makka informed Theodore, the brother of Heraclius, about the Muslim advance. Some historians allege that Heraclius himself was stationed at Ma'āb at this time and that his brother, Theodore, directed the Battle of Mu'ta. The Byzantines, aware of the Muslim approach, prepared a massive army.

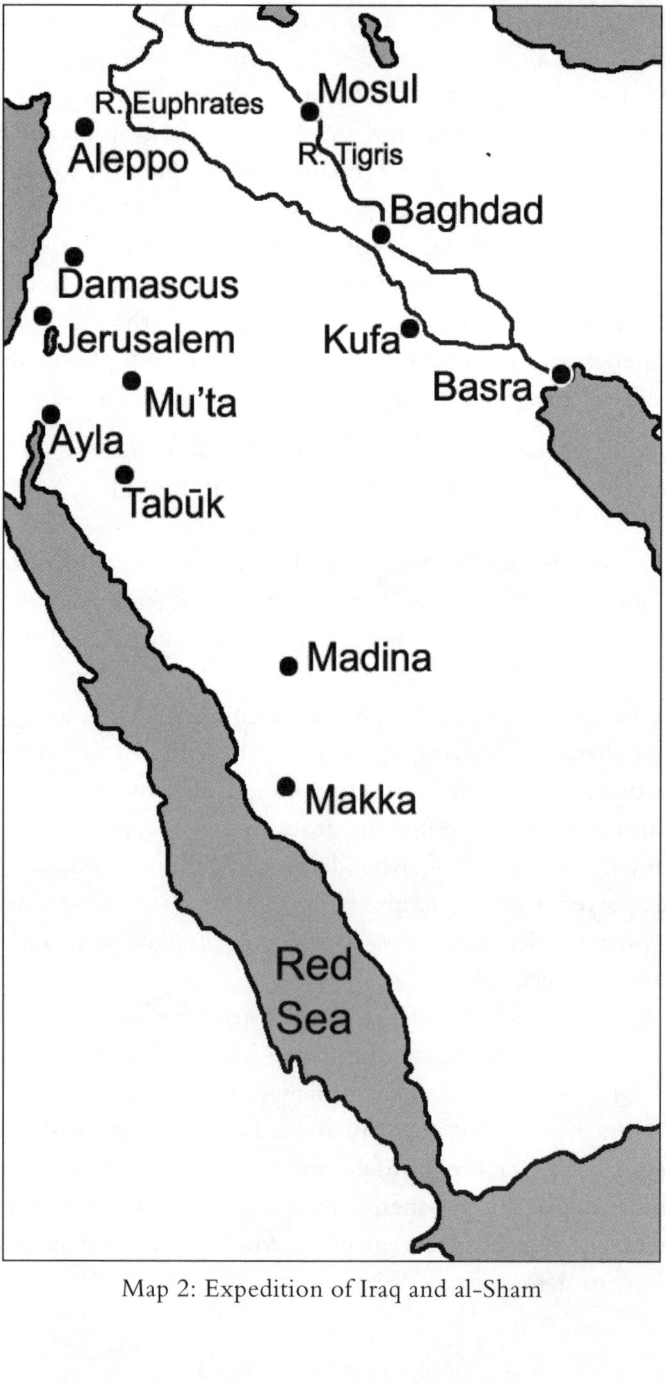

Map 2: Expedition of Iraq and al-Sham

The Muslims encamped at Maʿan, where through intelligence sources they received news that the Byzantines had assembled an army of over one hundred thousand, with joint forces from the tribes of Lakham, Judham, Qayn, Bahrā' and Balī.[8] For two days and nights the Muslims deliberated on the course of action in the face of such a superior enemy. A resolution was about to be passed, to inform the Prophet Muḥammad ﷺ on the situation and wait for either reinforcements or further counsel, when ʿAbdullāh ibn Rawāḥa ؓ intervened to encourage the *Ṣaḥāba*, he said:

> O people! By Allah, that which you fear might happen to you is precisely why you have come here – namely, martyrdom. We Muslims do not fight either with numbers, physical strength, or material equipment. Our only power lies in this religion that Allah has been gracious enough to give to us. Rise to battle and march forward! One of the two greatest blessings must befall you: either victory or martyrdom.[9]

The eloquent speech stirred the *Ṣaḥāba* to renewed determination to confront the Byzantines. Finally, in the year 8 at the village of Mu'ta, the three thousand Muslims faced the great Byzantine army, which had the most sophisticated armour and weapons of the day. The commander Zayd ؓ moved forward and he fought with great zeal, but the overwhelming numbers of the highly trained enemy claimed him. Jaʿfar ؓ picked up the banner, jumped off his horse and hamstrung her.[10] It was reported that in the battle Jaʿfar first lost his left arm, then carried the banner in the right, before losing his right arm also, then he grasped the banner between his legs and was martyred. ʿAbdullāh ibn ʿUmar ؓ further recalled, 'I was present amongst them in that battle and we searched for Jaʿfar ؓ and found his body amongst the bodies of the martyred ones. There were over ninety wounds on his body caused by stabs or shots of arrows.'[11] Thereafter 'Abdullāh ibn Rawāḥa ☙ carried the banner, whilst reciting the following couplet:

> I swear, my soul, you shall come to the battle
> You shall fight or be made to fight.
> Though men shout and scream aloud,
> Why should you spurn Paradise?
> Long have you been at ease.
> You are nothing but created from a drop in a worn out skin!

The battle claimed all three commanders. The events of the Battle of Mu'ta were simultaneously 'visually' unfolding to the Prophet ☙ in Madina, who in turn informed the people around him. It is reported on the authority of Anas ☙, that the Prophet ☙ had informed the people of the martyrdom of Zayd ☙, Ja'far ☙ and Ibn Rawāḥa ☙ before the news of their death reached them from the battlefield. The Prophet ☙ said, 'Zayd took the flag (as the commander of the army) and was martyred, then Ja'far took it and was martyred, and then Ibn Rawāḥa took it and was martyred.' While he spoke, his eyes were shedding tears.[12]

Facing annihilation, the Muslims nevertheless rallied and offered the command to Khālid ibn al-Walīd ☙. He obliged and at the eleventh hour effected a military miracle, by a brilliantly organized retreat that saved the army from total destruction. In Madina the Prophet ☙ informed the people: 'Then the flag was taken by a sword of Allah (i.e. Khālid) and Allah made them victorious.'[13] This was the battle in which the Muslims did not win the day but yet won the future through the tactical genius of Khālid ibn al-Walīd ☙ 'the Sword of Allah'.

Meanwhile, Heraclius carried on with his grand journey to have the prestige of returning the 'True Cross' to Jerusalem, where an orchestrated and gigantic fiesta was held in March

629. Heraclius' mind was not, however, far from conniving schemes to annihilate Madina. Though he had not witnessed the Battle of Mu'ta, he was certainly informed of it and the whispering of sweet revenge by the Ghassānids must have urged revenge.

By comparison with the great Persian Empire, putting down a few thousand Muslims in Madina must have seemed a minor foray. Heraclius must have started building up a military programme in al-Sham, and to this effect, in 9/630 rumours started pouring into Madina of a strong military build up of the Byzantine army on the northern frontier, around Tabūk.

Tabūk was a town strategically positioned between Damascus and Madina. The possibility of an attack on Madina was very real since the outcome of the Battle of Mu'ta had been inconclusive. Moreover, senior commanders, including Heraclius himself, who had just returned the Cross to Jerusalem, were still in al-Sham. The Prophet ﷺ accordingly called upon his Companions to come forward and march on Tabūk to check the Byzantine advance.

It was the month of Rajab and the heat was intense. The people were hard pressed because Madina was experiencing a severe drought. It was also the season for harvesting what little crops and fruits had survived. Exceptionally the Prophet ﷺ publicly declared the purpose and destination of the expedition prior to marching out of Madina. Until then, it had been his custom to announce an expedition without indicating its destination.

The reason given by most historians is that this allowed the *Ṣaḥāba* to prepare for an exceptionally arduous journey in a difficult season against a numerically superior enemy. Another reason is that the Muslims were going to defend against an expected attack, thereby eliminating the need for secrecy. Because of the hardship experienced by the *Ṣaḥāba*, this expedition is also referred to as *Al-'Usra* (the expedition of hardship).

The Prophet ﷺ had issued a call to defend the religion and the *Ṣaḥāba* responded in large numbers. However, in this expedition, the *Munāfiqūn* (the hypocrites), who had entered Islam either for their own advantage or to work against the Muslims from within, behaved as Allah willed for them. They exposed themselves by refusing to undertake what appeared to them a perilous expedition across the burning hot Arabian Desert without adequate provisions or equipment. The treacherous ones attempted to dissuade the believers from assisting the Prophet ﷺ. Regarding them, Allah revealed a verse:

> *Let them laugh a little: much will they weep: a recompense for what they do.* (al-Tawba 9: 82)

Others presented lame excuses. Jadd ibn Qays said: 'Will you allow me to stay behind and not tempt me, for everyone knows that I am strongly attracted to women and I am afraid that if I see the Byzantine women I shall not be able to control myself.' The Prophet ﷺ granted him exemption, but regarding him Allah revealed:

> *And among them is a man who says, 'Grant me exemption and draw me not into trial.' Have they not fallen into trial already? And indeed Hell surrounds the unbelievers.* (al-Tawba 9: 49)

Thousands of Muslims came forward. They were the ones who feared for the Hereafter, who believed that having Allah on their side was more important than all the comforts of this life. They assembled before the Prophet ﷺ to be led forward. Some supplied provisions and armour for their colleagues. Pre-eminent among them was Abū Bakr ؓ who contributed all his wealth. When the Prophet ﷺ asked him: 'What did you leave behind for your family,' he replied: 'I have left for them Allah and His Prophet.' ʿUmar ؓ, who brought half of all his wealth, admitted that he could never surpass Abū Bakr ؓ in his sacrifice for the cause of Islam. ʿUthmān ؓ is said to have taken the responsibility of supplying the needs of one-third of the army. Ibn Isḥāq states no one had ever spent like him. Ibn Hishām says that ʿUthmān ؓ had spent one thousand dinars on this expedition.'

The devoted Muslims desired earnestly to take part in the defence of Islam. A group of seven poor Muslims wept when they discovered there were no mounts or armour for them. They became known as 'The Weepers'. Their plight and burning desire to accompany the Prophet Muḥammad ﷺ on the expedition was answered when Yamīn b. ʿUmayr provided them with some food and one camel, which they could take turns to ride.

The Prophet ﷺ appointed ʿAlī ibn Abī Ṭālib ؓ[14] as his deputy during his absence from Madina. ʿAlī ؓ felt rather dejected and some reports say the Hypocrites spread false rumours, to the effect that ʿAlī ؓ was being left behind because he was a burden to the Prophet Muḥammad ﷺ.[15] Evidently affected by these rumours, ʿAlī ؓ called on the Prophet ﷺ and asked, 'Do you want to leave me with the children and women?' The Prophet ﷺ replied: 'Will you not be pleased that you will be to me like Aaron was to Moses ﵇? However, there will be no Prophet after me.'

As the defenders of Islam converged on Madina, their great number filled the town. Balādhurī[16] states that around 30,000 Muslims assembled making it the largest gathering thus far in the history of Islam. Children and others who could not join the expedition climbed trees and rooftops to wave farewell to the army and pray for their safe return. The Prophet ﷺ himself led the army. The sight of this great brotherhood of believers going out into the desert heat, risking their lives for the faith against the might of the Byzantine force, must surely have inspired those who, until then, had hesitated to join to now change their minds. One of these waverers was Abū Khaythama رضي الله عنه. On returning home, after the army had departed, he found his two wives in huts within his garden of palm trees surrounded by a fence. Each had sprinkled her hut with water to dampen the heat, and prepared cool drinking water and food for him. He stood at the entrance and looked at the comfort that awaited him. He said: 'The Messenger of Allah ﷺ is exposed to the heat of the sun and the blowing of the winds, while Abū Khaythama is in cool shade, with cool water, prepared food, and rests with a pretty woman in his estate. This is not just.'[17] Then he added: 'By Allah, I will not enter either of your huts, but will join the Messenger of Allah ﷺ, so get some provisions ready for me.' With haste he departed to join the Prophet ﷺ. On the way he met ʿUmayr b. Wahb رضي الله عنه. They travelled together, catching up with the Prophet ﷺ in Tabuk. Abū Khaythama رضي الله عنه informed the Prophet ﷺ what had happened and the Prophet ﷺ spoke kindly to him and invoked blessings upon him. [*see* Map 2]

On the march to Tabūk several *Ṣaḥāba* through tiredness began to lag behind. On one occasion the Companions indicated to the Prophet ﷺ that Abū Dharr رضي الله عنه had fallen behind. He said, 'Let him be, for if there is any good in him Allah will join him to you. If not, Allah will relieve you of him.' When the Prophet Muḥammad ﷺ pitched camp, and onlookers called his attention to a lonely man walking towards them, the Prophet ﷺ said that he wished it would be Abū Dharr رضي الله عنه. When the people confirmed this, the Prophet ﷺ said, 'May Allah have mercy on Abū Dharr! He walks alone, will die alone,[18] and will be raised alone.'

On route the army passed the ruins of Thamūd[19] at a place called al-Ḥijr. Ibn ʿUmar reported that when the Prophet ﷺ

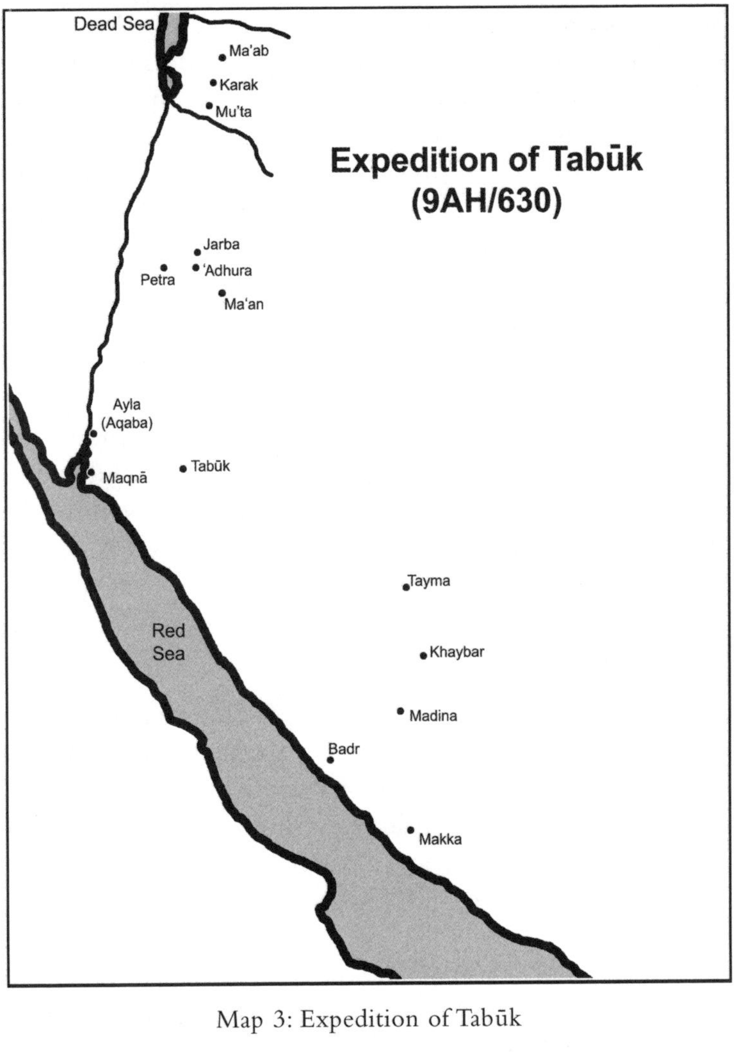

Map 3: Expedition of Tabūk

passed by al-Ḥijr, he said: 'Do not enter the dwelling places of those who were unjust to themselves, unless you enter in a weeping state lest the same calamity as theirs should befall you.' Then he covered his head and sped off across the valley.[20] The Prophet ﷺ further ordered: 'Do not drink any of its water nor perform ablution with it. If you have used it for making dough, then eat none of it, but feed it to the camels. Let none of you go out at night except with a companion.'

Before the Prophet ﷺ reached Tabūk, the Byzantines had taken stock of the situation and decided the time was not right to confront the Muslims. Hence, they retreated into their own territories. The Prophet ﷺ had no intention of pursuing the Byzantines. His objective, to secure the frontiers, had been achieved without loss of life and he was content. Having travelled all the way to Tabūk, and as a routine practice, he invited the leaders of the neighbouring tribes to embrace Islam or pay the *jizya*.[21]

Yuḥannā b. Ru'ba, governor of Ayla (a seaport at the end of the Gulf), came to him, made a treaty and offered to pay the *jizya*. The tribes of Jarbā' (a fortress situated on the Roman road leading from Buṣrā to the Red Sea) and ʿAdhura (a Byzantine camp between Maʿan and Petra) also agreed to pay the *jizya*. The Prophet ﷺ wrote a document for each of them:

> In the name of Allah, the Merciful, the Compassionate. This is a covenant of security granted under Allah by Muḥammad, the Prophet of Allah, to Yuḥannā b. Ru'ba and the people of Ayla. Their ships, vehicles, and routes on land and on sea are secure under Allah's guaranty and Muḥammad's. So are all those who accompany them whether of the people of al-Sham, Yemen, or beyond the seas. Whoever among them perpetrates a crime shall be liable for it in his own person, and it shall be legitimate for Muḥammad to confiscate his wealth. It shall not be legitimate to prevent any one of them from using a well or a road on land or sea which they have been in the habit of using.[22]

Similar documents were presented to the tribes of Jarbā' and ʿAdhura, who offered to pay 100 dinars per annum, and to the people of Maqnā, who offered to pay in goods one-fourth of the fish they caught, horses, coats-of-mail, and fruits. The people of Ayla paid one dinar per person, making it 300 dinars per annum in all.

After the work of inviting the people and local dignitaries was done, the Prophet Muḥammad ﷺ ordered Khālid ibn al-Walīd ؓ to find and arrest Ukhaydir ibn ʿAbd al-Malik in Dūmat al-Jandal.[23] Ukhaydir was a Christian and close associate of the Byzantines, with a known hatred for Islam. He was likely to join forces with the Byzantines for a possible attack on Madina. The Prophet ﷺ therefore deemed it necessary in order to be secure from such an attack either to win over or subdue Ukhaydir.

The Muslim cavalry were fortunate to encounter Ukhaydir and his brother in a hunting party outside the gates of Dūmat al-Jandal on a moonlit night. Khālid ؓ attacked the hunting party, and seized Ukhaydir, whose brother was killed in the skirmish. A silk robe woven with gold was captured[24] and sent to Madina by Khālid ؓ, which arrived before him. The Companions began to touch and marvel at the quality of the cloth.

Al-Barā' ؓ said, 'A silk robe was presented to the Prophet Muḥammad ﷺ and his Companions began to touch it and marvel at its softness. Then he said: "Do you marvel at the softness of this? Saʿd ibn Muʿādh's[25] headband in paradise is better and softer than it."'[26]

Ukhaydir was presented to the Prophet ﷺ by Khālid ؓ. The Prophet spared his life and invited him to Islam. Ukhaydir accepted and became an ally and was later reinstated as the leader of his people.[27]

Upon the Prophet's ﷺ return to Madina, as was his *sunna* (the Prophet's way) after returning home from a journey, he went to the mosque and offered two *rakʿa ṣalāh* (units of prayer). Thereafter, he received the people. From those who had stayed behind, the Hypocrites came forward first, offered (false) excuses and took oaths before him. The Prophet Muḥammad ﷺ accepted their excuses, took their pledge of allegiance and asked Allah's forgiveness for them, and left the secrets of their hearts for Allah to judge.[28] Amongst the faithful believers who had not made the journey was Kaʿb ibn Mālik ؇.[29]

The Prophet ﷺ ordered the Companions to boycott Kaʿb ibn Mālik ؇ and two other Muslims, Murāra ibn al-Rabīʿ al-ʿAmrī ؇ and Hilāl ibn Umayya al-Wāqifī ؇, who had also failed to join the expedition.

Kaʿb ؇ said: 'The people stopped talking to us and the very land where I lived appeared strange to me as if I did not know it.' Before forty days had elapsed a Nabaṭī (Christian farmer) from al-Sham asked people to lead him to Kaʿb ibn Mālik. They did so. The Nabaṭī handed Kaʿb a letter from the Chief of the Ghassanids. In it was written:

> I have been informed that your friend (the Prophet) has treated you harshly. Anyhow, Allah does not let you live at a place where you feel inferior and your right is lost. So join us, and we will console you.

Evidently, the Byzantine espionage was effective enough to have learned, within forty days, of the situation in Madina, and contemplated inducing Muslims to defect. The Muslims' knowledge of the Byzantines' sinister intents justified their unease and insecurity.

Kaʿb ؇ said, 'When I read the letter, I said to myself, "This is also a test." Then I took the letter to the oven and made a fire therein by burning it.'

The boycott continued and later the Prophet ﷺ ordered the three to abstain from cohabiting with their wives. The boycott lasted for a total of 50 days, after which Kaʿb and his colleagues were forgiven. (See appendix F for a full account of this story.)

Ka'b ibn Mālik's sincerity and honesty is merely an example of the *Ṣaḥāba*'s practices. The Prophet's quick and easy pardoning of the Hypocrites as compared with the devout Muslims is of profound importance. Ka'b ibn Mālik's resolute faith in the Prophet's judgement is a prime example of the community's obedience and respect for orders irrespective of the tempting propositions that might come from the enemies of Islam.

SECOND PHASE

On Monday the 12th of Rabīʿ al-Awwal 11/7th June 632, the beloved Prophet ﷺ left the worldly abode for Allah and Paradise. Before his departure he had ensured through treaties, as well as *daʿwa*, that the inhabitants of Arabia posed no threat to Islam. Plainly Islam was never going to be totally secure with the Byzantines close by in al-Sham. The Muslims were especially vulnerable to attack from the region of Mu'ta. To gain a first-hand appraisal of the situation, the Prophet Muḥammad ﷺ appointed Usāma ؓ, a young and dedicated twenty-year-old Companion to command a battalion and instructed him to undertake an expedition to the settlements bordering al-Sham.

He was to cover the territories of Balqā' and al-Dārūm,[30] in the land of Palestine. His duties included gathering intelligence, monitoring Byzantine manoeuvres, and trying to win over the local inhabitants.

Usāma ؓ was the son of Zayd ؓ, the commander of the battle of Mu'ta and the grandson of Ḥārith ؓ, the bearer of the Prophet's ﷺ letter, who had been murdered at Mu'ta. Prior to embarking on the long expedition into Palestine, the *Ṣaḥāba* gathered at Jurf (today known as Siqāyat Sulaymān), some three miles from Madina. Some *Ṣaḥāba* in the camp at Jurf were not at ease with the appointment of Usāma as commander. 'Umar ❊ was so alarmed at the disquiet amongst them, that he returned to Madina to report the matter to the Prophet ❊. The Prophet ❊ was angered by the news. Though he had been confined to bed due to illness, he came out of his apartment to address the people:

> O People! I have been informed about the criticism of some of you for appointing Usāma as the commander. By Allah, you have not only criticised the appointment of Usāma as the commander but also the appointment of his father when he was made commander before this. By Allah, he was fully able to be appointed as the commander and likewise his son has full ability for this command. He is most beloved to me among all the people as his father was most beloved to me among all the people. Both of them are the treasures of every type of goodness; you should also treat them well. He (Usāma) is among the selected ones.[31]

This was Saturday 10th of Rabī' al-Awwal. After the speech the Ṣaḥāba came forward to bid farewell and salāms to the Prophet ❊. Many volunteers came forward including eminent leading figures from both the Muhājirūn[32] and the Anṣār.[33] Just hours before the army's departure from Jurf, they received the devastating news of the Prophet's ❊ death.

The light that illuminated and guided their lives was no more. On hearing the news, they became like ships without sails. The commander's banner was rolled up and they began the three-mile journey back to Madina. Many in their grief, not believing or accepting the grim news, confronted others. Dare they say the Prophet ❊ had passed away? One amongst the many was 'Umar ❊, who could not accept the reality.

Ibn Isḥāq states that, when the Prophet of Allah ❊ passed away, 'Umar ❊ got up and said: 'Some of the disaffected will allege that the Prophet ﷺ has died, but by Allah, he is not dead. He has gone to his Lord as Moses ibn ʿImrān ؑ went and was hidden from his people for forty days, returning to them after it was said that he had died. By Allah, the Prophet ﷺ will return as Moses ؑ returned and will cut off the hands and feet of men who allege that the Prophet ﷺ is dead.'

When Abū Bakr ؓ heard the news he rushed to the Prophet's Mosque.[34] As he entered, he saw ʿUmar ؓ speaking to the people. He paid no attention to him and instead went into ʿĀ'isha's room[35] to the Prophet of Allah ﷺ, who was lying covered with a cloth. He uncovered his face and kissed him, saying: 'You are dearer to me than my father and mother. You have tasted the death, which Allah had decreed: a second death will never overtake you.' Then he replaced the cloth on the Prophet and went out. ʿUmar ؓ, deep in shock, was still warning people against thinking the Prophet ﷺ had died. Abū Bakr ؓ aware of the serious and delicate situation of the people, in their grief and anguish, went to one corner of the mosque and began to speak. When the *Ṣaḥāba* saw Abū Bakr ؓ wishing to address them, they gathered round him. He said:

'O People! If any one of you worshipped Muḥammad ﷺ he should know that Muḥammad ﷺ is dead. But those who worshipped Allah should know that He is Alive and will never die. Allah says in the Qur'ān: Muḥammad is only a Messenger of Allah. There came down a number of Messengers before him. Then would you turn back from Islam, if he dies or is killed?'[36]

ʿAbdullāh ibn ʿUmar ؓ says, 'It seemed that the verse of the Qur'ān which Abū Bakr ؓ referred to was just revealed, although we had recited it several times in the past.'

ʿUmar ؓ later commented, 'By Allah, when I heard Abū Bakr ؓ recite these words I was dumbfounded so that my legs could not bear me and I fell to the ground knowing that the Prophet of Allah ﷺ was indeed dead.'

The speech by Abū Bakr ﵁ defused the crisis. It calmed the people down and brought them to the bleak poignant reality of what had happened.

Its effectiveness and wisdom cannot be overstated.

Burayda ibn al-Ḥuṣayb ﵁ rolled-up the commander's banner, which had been conferred upon Usāma by the Prophet ﷺ and propped it up against the wall of the Prophet's house.

After the Prophet ﷺ passed away, Abū Bakr ﵁ was elected to be the first Caliph. In the very first hours of holding that office, he was called upon to make a crucial decision on behalf of Islam.

News of the Prophet's illness and subsequent death spread far and wide within days. From the episode of Kaʿb ﵁ after the expedition of Tabūk it can be ascertained that even the court of the Byzantine Emperor must have received notification within days. New converts whose faith was still weak started wavering. Apostates began to defy the authority of Madina, and there was a threat of attack on Muslims. Abū Bakr ﵁ was being severely tested. The eminent *Ṣaḥāba* called upon him and requested him not to despatch Usāma ﵁ on the expedition that the Prophet ﷺ had sanctioned. But Abū Bakr ﵁ was firm in his faith and replied: 'I swear by Him in Whose hands is my life that even if I knew for certain that I was going to be ravaged by wild beasts, I will still despatch Usāma.'

Having failed to persuade him to change his mind, the *Ṣaḥāba,* through ʿUmar ibn al-Khaṭṭāb ﵁, a very close companion of Abū Bakr ﵁, sought an alternative approach and requested a change of commander, for Usāma ﵁ was only twenty years of age and inexperienced. Abū Bakr ﵁ however, was not one to be moved. He replied: 'Thy mother be childless, O son of al-Khaṭṭāb! Shall the Prophet of Allah ﷺ appoint a man to the command and I depose him and appoint another in his place?' These very first decisions established the principle by which Abū Bakr was to govern the *Umma* (Muslim Community). The words of Allah from the Qur'ān and the ways shown by the Prophet ﷺ were to be the foremost principles employed in any policy to be undertaken. Throughout his life Abū Bakr remained steadfast on the *path of Islam* and did not deviate from it. His devotion to Islam is reflected brightly from his inaugural speech to the very end of his august life, a legacy surely unsurpassable. His statements concerning the weak and the strong, loyalty and treachery, are worthy of note. In particular his unswerving devotion to the adherence to Islamic principles is particularly noteworthy

Abū Bakr, after praising Allah said:

> I have been given authority over you but I am not the best among you. If I do well, help me, and if I do ill, then put me right. Truth consists in loyalty and falsehood in treachery. The weak among you shall be strong in my eyes until I secure his right if Allah wills: and the strong among you shall be weak in my eyes until I wrest the right from him. If a people refrain from striving in the way of Allah, Allah will smite them with disgrace. Wickedness is never widespread in a people but Allah brings calamity upon them all. Obey me as long as I obey Allah and His Prophet, and if I disobey them you owe me no obedience. Arise to prayer. Allah have mercy on you.

The Caliph ordered the army to march and accompanied the force for some distance. He went on foot while the young commander rode on horseback. Usāma begged Abū Bakr to be mounted, or he would walk as well. 'Not so', replied Abū Bakr. 'I will not mount. What harm is there if some dust falls on my feet. For every step in the way of the Lord is equal to the merit of manifold good works and erases a multitude of sins.'

The Caliph advised the army: 'Avoid treachery, depart not in any way from the right, mutilate none, kill no children, women, or aged men. Injure not, nor burn date or palm trees, which serve men or beast. Slay not any flocks or herds or camels save for sustenance. If the monks submit leave them alone. Now march forward in the name of the Lord and may He protect you.'

He then prayed for them: 'I entrust to Allah your religion, your tryst and the end of your deeds.'

The expansion into the Byzantine territories by the Muslims has given rise to many theories. It has been explained as a need to control and direct outwards military might, to gain land and wealth. Islamic principles are very clear on the need for, and manner of, waging war. One cannot imagine that the Companions of the Prophet ﷺ, especially under the command of Abū Bakr ؓ, ʿUmar ؓ, ʿUthmān ؓ and ʿAlī ؓ, when most expansion took place, would deviate from the principles of Islamic teachings.

Shaykh Saʿdī in his *Bustān* says:

> When it is possible to take the country with gentleness,
> In contest, bring not forth blood from a single pore of the body
> In the name of manliness! Because, the country of the whole earth
> Is not worth one drop of blood that trickles on the earth.
> I heard that King Jamshid of happy nature
> Wrote on a stone, at a fountain head.
> 'At this fountain, many like us took rest;
> They departed (in death), just as the eyes twinkled.
> With manliness and force, they took the world;
> But, they took it not with themselves to the tomb.'

Thus Usāma ؓ left three weeks after the Prophet's death. Originally ʿUmar ؓ was designated to be a member of the expedition but Abū Bakr ؓ sought Usāma's permission to leave him behind in Madina and, accordingly, permission was granted.

Usāma ؓ marched stage by stage until he reached Mu'ta, where his father's death was avenged. After approximately two months on the Byzantine frontiers he returned to Madina with his mission accomplished.

To put things into perspective we need to note the following dates: the Battle of Mu'ta took place sometime in 8/September 629. Early in the following year, 9/March 630, Heraclius visited Jerusalem and passed through Mu'ta. Some historians claim that the Ghassānids requested Heraclius to attack Madina on this occasion. However, Heraclius' prestige and glory lay in returning the 'True Cross' to Jerusalem and so he postponed the attack. He was still in al-Sham when the Prophet ﷺ after receiving information of a possible attack on Madina, undertook the expedition to Tabūk. This was during late 9/late 630 early 631. Thus, in 12/July/August 632, when Usāma ؓ was sent out to secure the north-west flank of the peninsula, the Byzantines had organized their military machine and command. Further, the Jews expelled from Arabia had settled in the region of Palestine and were actively inciting hatred against Madina. Usāma ؓ must, therefore, have faced considerable opposition.

Usāma's ؓ successful foray must have sent shock waves to the heart of the Byzantine Empire. It also discouraged any possible attack on Madina by the apostates. Those who contemplated attacking Madina reconsidered their position for they had been led to believe, incorrectly, that Abū Bakr ؓ must have had a large enough reserve army in Madina to send Usāma ؓ on such a dangerous expedition. The Jews and Christian Arabs along the border who had allied with the Byzantines were also subdued. This was another of the numerous prudent decisions that Abū Bakr ﷺ was to take during his illustrious two years as Caliph.

The remaining months of the year 632 were spent subduing the apostates. These efforts are called the *Ridda* wars. While the Muslims were busy in the Ḥijāz with the apostates, the northern and western flanks of the border with al-Sham witnessed random plundering raids by nomadic groups allied to the Byzantines. The Muslims living along the borders with al-Sham were regularly falling victim to these raids and losing livestock to the Byzantine confederates. Travelling along the western borders became hazardous for the Muslims on account of these bandits, allied to and supported by the Byzantines. It would appear that Islam initially had great difficulty in breaching the system of political alliance established by the Byzantines.

THIRD PHASE

At this point, some five years had passed since Heraclius defeated the Persians. The Byzantines had sufficient time to re-establish control over their territories and direct their military energy and expansionist interests towards Madina. The skirmishes along the borders were only one aspect of the threats the Muslims encountered.

Abū Bakr ﷺ, having weighed up the grave situation, put forward a proposal for the need to protect the Syrian/Byzantine frontier. He normally decided matters of state after consultation and accordingly, called a special *Shūrā* (Council of Advisors) to discuss the matter. Although the selection or election of this council did not take place by public voting, the prominent figures in the *Shūrā* were the most popular and respected figures in the community. Membership of the *Shūrā* was not based upon colour, race, wealth or worldly power. It was based upon services rendered to Islam and closeness to Allah and His Prophet ﷺ.[37]

Ibn Saʿd has recorded that whenever Abū Bakr ؓ faced a problem he summoned the eminent *Muhājirūn* and *Anṣār*. The following persons were permanent members of the *Shūrā*: ʿUmar ؓ, ʿUthmān ؓ, ʿAlī ؓ, ʿAbdur Raḥmān ibn ʿAwf ؓ,[38] Muʿādh ibn Jabal ؓ,[39] Ubayy ibn Kaʿb ؓ[40] and Zayd ibn Thābit ؓ.[41] On certain occasions wider consultation took place to which all prominent Companions were called.

On this occasion Abū Bakr ؓ called ʿAlī ؓ, ʿUmar ؓ, ʿUthmān ؓ, ʿAbdur Raḥmān ibn ʿAwf ؓ, Saʿd ibn Abī Waqqāṣ ؓ, Saʿīd ibn Zayd ؓ, Abū ʿUbayda ibn al-Jarrāḥ ؓ and all the other *Muhājirūn* and *Anṣār*. Abū Bakr ؓ addressed them:

'Verily the favours of Allah, the Exalted, the Sublime, are countless. The good deeds cannot substitute those favours. Therefore, all praises are due to Allah. It is Allah Who united your word for you, reformed your affairs, guided you towards Islam and removed the evil effects of Satan from you. Now the Satan has lost all the hope that you would associate partners with Allah; and worship another god besides Allah. All the Arabs are like children of one father and mother today. I think that the Muslims should go to fight the Romans in al-Sham and Allah will help the Muslims: and Allah's word will certainly be exalted. The Muslims would get enormous virtues from the Holy War as whosoever amongst them will be killed, will be counted as a martyr. There is great goodness with Allah for the righteous ones. While whosoever will survive, will be treated as the great *Mujāhid* (Struggler for the cause of Islam) in the cause of Allah. This is my opinion which has come to my thoughts. Now you should give your opinion on the matter.'[42]

One by one the Companions expressed their opinion and all were in agreement with Abū Bakr ؓ. One typical response was from ʿAlī ؓ: 'I feel you will gain victory over them whether you lead the army yourself or send it under someone else's command, *Inshā' Allāh* (Allah willing).'

Abū Bakr ؓ further asked him, 'May Allah be pleased with you, but how do you know about this?' ʿAlī ؓ replied, 'I have heard the Prophet ﷺ say, "This religion will always overcome the one who opposes it and has a grudge against it. Afterwards this religion (Islam) will be well established and its followers will gain an upper hand."'

Abū Bakr ؓ remarked, '*Subḥānallāh* (Glory to Allah)! You have made a pleasant remark. May Allah be pleased with you.'

Thereafter Abū Bakr ؓ stood up and addressed the people:

'O, people! Certainly Allah has bestowed His favours upon you by guiding you towards Islam, has honoured you with the *jihād* and has exalted this religion above the other religions. O servants of Allah! Now prepare for the war with the Romans in al-Sham.'[43]

Khālid ibn Saʿīd ؓ (different from Khālid the *sword of Allah*) declared his willingness to assume command. He was fifth among the male Muslims to accept Islam. He was a trusted Companion of the Prophet ﷺ and had been stationed in Yemen. During the *Ridda* wars he returned to Madina. After being appointed as the commander, he proceeded to the Syrian front. His mission entailed several undertakings: he was sent to Tayma, an oasis village near the Syrian border *en route* to Damascus. His initial objective was to serve as a protective barrier against the large concentration of hostile forces, made up of local tribes, which had been strategically assembled by the Byzantines with the real possibility of striking into the Ḥijāz. He was also required to gather intelligence about the Byzantine military and, no doubt, to protect the local villages along the border against raids by the nomads allied to the Byzantines. What he was not directed to do was enter Syrian territory. All historians agree that Khālid ibn Saʿīd's ؓ mission was defensive rather than offensive.

To this effect Abū Bakr ﷺ wrote a letter stating: 'Continue your march cautiously, do not go too far across the border of al-Sham lest the enemy may fall upon you from the back.'[44]

Khālid ibn Saʿīd ﷺ was further advised not to confront any Syrian forces unless attacked. Upon Khālid's approach to the borders of al-Sham, the Byzantines executed a cunning manoeuvre. They attacked the Muslims with very light infantry whom Khālid ﷺ was easily able to defeat. Over-confident with the ease of his victory, he marched forward into al-Sham only to be trapped in a well-planned ambush. Khālid's forces were encircled and faced a humiliating defeat. Khālid ibn Saʿīd ﷺ escaped. ʿIkrima ﷺ[45] stayed with the troops to offer rearguard protection. Upon receiving the news, without any delay Abū Bakr ﷺ despatched a letter to Khālid ﷺ, stating:

Remain where you are (i.e. do not return to Madina). By my life, you are as fast in receding your steps as you are quick in marching forward against the enemy. You run away from the battlefield when confronted with difficulties, you do not face the enemy resolutely till victory.[46]

Islam was now under direct threat from the Byzantines. Abū Bakr ﷺ alarmed at the possibility of an imminent attack, recalled the eminent Companions for consultation. The urgent and pressing task was to reinforce the remnants of Khālid ibn Saʿīd's force.

An effective response required the assembly of a large enough army to face the mighty Byzantines. Initially, people from the Ḥijāz region were encouraged to participate, but it soon became apparent that more were needed. Abū Bakr ﷺ therefore wrote to the Arab tribe of Ṭayyi' in the Najd and to the Yemen. His message read:

> *In the name of Allah, All compassionate and Most Merciful.* From the Caliph of the Prophet ﷺ to all Muslims of Yemen. Salutations to those whom this letter is read over. I praise Allah besides whom there is none worthy

> of worship. Allah has made *jihād* incumbent upon Muslims and has commanded that whether they be in ease or in hardened strait, they should sally forth and strive with their lives and wealth in the way of Allah. *Jihād* is a confirmed obligation and its reward is immense. I have exhorted Muslims to come out for holy war with the Romans in al-Sham and they have splendidly responded with sincerity and steadfastness of purpose. O servants of the Lord! You should also participate with alacrity and sincerity in the enterprise the Muslims have embarked upon. You will not be denied one of the two rewards. Either you will die a martyr's death or gain victory and spoils of war. Verily, in the sight of Allah profession is naught without action. The obligation of *jihād* will continue to be imposed so long as the enemies of Allah do not accept the faith and decree of the book of the Lord. May Allah establish for you your religion, enlighten your hearts, cleanse your deeds and bestow upon you the reward of the patient and the striving.[47]

The scarcity of manpower was acute and Abū Bakr's ﷺ recruitment effort was directed to all corners of the Peninsula.

It was again a wise decision by Abū Bakr ﷺ to check the Byzantines at this early insecure stage of Islam, because within Arabia the apostates had just been subdued and others who refused to pay the *zakāh* were being checked. On the eastern front the Muslims, under the command of Khālid ibn al-Walīd ﷺ, were engaged in battle with the Persian forces. The Muslims were stretched on all fronts. However, following Khālid ibn Saʿīd's defeat, the threat of an attack by the Byzantines made it incumbent to respond quickly and firmly.

Thus Abū Bakr ﷺ began to gather the Muslims. The acute shortage of manpower was reflected in the fact that only 24,000 were assembled to face the mighty legions of the Byzantine

Empire. All historians are unanimous on the fact that an army of twenty-four thousand people was gathered. It included more than one thousand *Ṣaḥāba*, of whom about one hundred had participated in the Battle of Badr. Four commanders were chosen: ʿAmr ibn al-ʿĀṣ,[48] Yazīd ibn Abī Sufyān[49] (replacing Khālid ibn Saʿīd), Abū ʿUbayda ibn al-Jarrāḥ[50] and Shuraḥbīl ibn Ḥasana.[51]

Before the appointment of the leaders, each was asked if they would assume command. ʿAmr ibn al-ʿĀṣ held a prestigious position overseeing the taxation of the northwest Ḥijāz, a position to which the Prophet ﷺ had appointed him and Abū Bakr reinstated him after his expedition to Oman. Abū Bakr wrote to ʿAmr, saying:

'While complying with the promise of the Prophet ﷺ, I have re-appointed you to the post that was given to you by the Prophet of Allah ﷺ prior to sending you to Oman. Now once again you are in the same desired job. I would like, Abū ʿAbdullāh, to devote you entirely to that which is better for you in your present life and your Hereafter, unless that which you have now is preferable to you.'

ʿAmr ibn ʿĀṣ, without a second thought, responded speedily to the service of Islam: 'I am but an arrow in the quiver of Islam, and you the archer. It is for you to pick out the fittest shaft, and aim against the enemy.'

The Muslim army was divided into four groups. The participants from the Battle of Badr were given the freedom to join the commander of their choice. The commanders were asked to respect the Badr comrades and take counsel from them. They in turn were requested to respect the commands of their respective leader.

Abū Bakr reminded the people:

> Every affair has factors that bring it together. Whoever reaches an understanding of them, they suffice him. Whoever works for Allah, Allah protects him. You must

> work earnestly and deliberately, for forethought is more likely to accomplish goals. Is it not the case that anyone who has no faith has no religion, that whoever has no account of good deeds gets no goodly reward, and that whoever has no intention has no reward for his work. Indeed, the reward in Allah's book for *jihād* in Allah's path is something for which a Muslim should love to be singled out, by which Allah has saved people from humiliation, and through which Allah has bestowed nobility in this world and the next.[52]

According to Ibn Isḥāq, ʿAmr ibn al-ʿĀṣ ﷺ was directed towards Palestine. He travelled from Madina along the coastal route to the tip of the Gulf of ʿAqaba via the village of Ayla into Palestine. ʿAmr's forces during the initial part camped at Ghamr al-Arabat. This is located between the Dead Sea and the Gulf of ʿAqaba along the Wādi Araba. Yazīd ibn Abī Sufyān ﷺ, Shuraḥbīl ibn Ḥasana ﷺ and Abū ʿUbayda ﷺ marched via the Tabūk road towards al-Sham. Yazīd ibn Abī Sufyān ﷺ was sent to the Balqa region, east and northeast of the Dead Sea. Shuraḥbīl ibn Ḥasana ﷺ was directed towards present-day Jordan. Abū ʿUbayda ﷺ entered the Golan Heights to the south of Damascus.

Al-Ṭabarī[53] records a slightly different account in the movements of the commanders. He reports that, ʿAmr ﷺ took the coastal route and Abū ʿUbayda ﷺ followed the same path and branched out later on the journey. Yazīd ﷺ and Shuraḥbīl ibn Ḥasana ﷺ took the Tabūk route with Shuraḥbīl ﷺ taking charge of Khālid ibn Saʿīd's forces. Al-Ṭabarī states, Abū Bakr ﷺ directed one column to descend and the other to ascend and vice versa. This would appear to mean that they fanned out and criss-crossed to fill in the gaps along the front so that the different divisions could support one another more easily in the event of a Byzantine counter-attack.

Shuraḥbīl ibn Ḥasana, Yazīd ibn Abī Sufyān, and Abū ʿUbayda according to al-Madā'inī, set out with 7,000 men each, and ʿAmr ibn al-ʿĀṣ marched with 3,000 men. According to Balādhurī, each of the commanders had 3,000 men under his leadership, but Abū Bakr kept on sending reinforcements until the total built up to 24,000.

According to Balādhurī, this took place in Ṣafar 13/633-634. (See pp. 71-72.)

Abū Bakr escorted each of the generals in turn for a short distance on foot as he had done nearly two years earlier with Usāma. He gave his final counsel and prayed for them. To ʿAmr ibn al-ʿĀṣ (transmitted by Ibn Saʿd) he said:

> O ʿAmr! Keep fearing Allah in public and private. Keep feeling shy of Him, for He looks upon you and your acts.You have already seen that I have given you preference to those who are ahead of you with respect to good acts and wealth among the Muslims: hence you become one who acts keeping the Hereafter before him, and what you do should be meant for the pleasure of Allah: act as a father to those who depend on you: do not be on the look out for others' secrets: never be careless about your duties: fight with your enemies with righteousness and never act cowardly: do not indulge in embezzlement: punish the embezzlers: do not admonish your friends in lengthy terms: rectify yourself and your subjects will turn good.

To Yazīd ibn Abī Sufyān, Abū Bakr said:

> O Yazīd! You will soon arrive in a country where the people will bring you all kinds of food, so utter the name of Allah at the beginning and at the end. Further, you will come across people who have secluded themselves in convents; leave them and their seclusion

> (i.e. churches or monasteries). But you will come across people on whose heads the devil has taken his abode (the Shamāmisa) so strike their heads off. But do not kill any old man or woman or minor or sick person or monk. Do not devastate any population. Do not cut a tree except for some useful purpose. Do not burn a palm-tree nor inundate it. Do not commit treachery, do not mutilate, do not show cowardice, and do not cheat. Allah shall surely give victory to those who help His cause and also to His Messenger ﷺ, for Allah is Strong and Powerful. I commit you to the care of Allah, and bid you farewell.[54]

The Muslims' most effective weapon as they marched into the Byzantine territories was their understanding and practice of Islam. It is this commitment, and not material valour alone, that opened the way for them. They adhered fully to the Islamic code of conduct in warfare and in their daily dealings. Every *mujāhid* was conscious of his actions and conduct and aware of the Qur'ān's many injunctions to this effect. In particular:

> *Say: Shall I seek for (my) Cherisher other than Allah, when He is the Cherisher of all things (that exist)? Every soul draws the meed of its acts on none but itself: no bearer of burdens can bear the burden of another. Your goal in the end is towards Allah: He will tell you the truth of the things wherein you disputed.* (al-Anʿam 6: 164)

> *Nor can a bearer of burdens bear another's burden. If one heavily laden should call another to (bear) his load, not the least portion of it can be carried (by the other), even though he be near related. You can only admonish such as fear their Lord unseen and establish regular prayer. And whoever purifies himself does so for the benefit of his own soul; and the destination (of all) is to Allah.* (al-Fāṭir 35: 18)

Not only did the *Ṣaḥāba* advance with the purpose of defending the borders of Ḥijāz but they were also the finest ambassadors of Islam the world has ever seen, and with these dual responsibilities they marched forward in the name of the Lord and for the sake of Islam and confronted the Byzantines.

NOTES

1. Maulānā Muḥammad Yūsuf Kāndhlawī, *Ḥayātus Ṣaḥāba, The Lives of the Companions of the Prophet* (New Delhi, 1987), Vol. I, p. 134.
2. Zayd, prior to Islam, was a slave of Khadīja, the first wife of the Prophet Muḥammad ﷺ. She freed him and the Prophet ﷺ adopted him as his son. The Prophet ﷺ arranged his marriage to his own cousin Zaynab bint Jahsh. Zayd is one of a few Companions referred to in the Qur'ān. (See *Sūra al-Aḥzāb* 33: 4.)
3. *Ṣaḥīḥ* Muslim, *Ḥadīth* 5958, Vol. 4, p. 1294, trans. Abdul Hamid Siddiqi, *Kitāb Bhavan*, New Delhi, India, 1987.
4. Jaʿfar was the first cousin of the Prophet ﷺ. He was in the group of Companions who made the first *Ḥijra* (migration) to Ethiopia from Makka. He is credited with the eloquent address to the Ethiopian King that secured their position and upon which the King is said to have accepted Islam. In 7 he rejoined the Muslims in Madina.
5. ʿAbdullāh was a renowned poet and trusted Companion. He made two raids on Khaybar and after its conquest was put in charge of assessing and collecting tax revenue. His eloquent speech prior to the Battle of Mu'ta was a decisive factor in inspiring the valour of the Muslims.
6. Bukhārī, *Kitāb al-Jāmiʿ al-Ṣaḥīḥ*, ed. M. Ludolf Krehl. Leiden, 1862-1908, Vol. 2, p. 251.
7. Khālid ؓ was born 17 years prior to Islam to the Banū Makhzūm tribe of the Quraysh. Prior to accepting Islam he was an ardent enemy and played a pivotal role in the limited success of the polytheists at the Battle of Uḥud. Upon accepting Islam, after the truce of Ḥudaybiya, he laboured earnestly in the cause of Islam. The Prophet ﷺ honoured him with the title, 'the Sword of Allah' for his courage and genius as a commander. He served in Arabia, Iraq and al-Sham and was prominent in all the major battles of Islam in his lifetime. He settled in Ḥimṣ, al-Sham, where he died in 21. He appointed the Caliph ʿUmar ibn al-Khaṭṭāb ؓ, as the trustee for his property.
8. Maulānā Muḥammad Yūsuf Kāndhlawī, op. cit., p. 686.

9. Haykal, Muhammad Hussain, *The Life of Muhammad* (North American Trust Publ., 1976), p. 389.

10. Ja'far was the first man in Islam to hamstring his horse, an act, under the conditions, which was certain to lead to his death (see Ibn Isḥāq).

11. Bukhārī, Vol. V, *Ḥadīth* 560, p. 392.

12. Ibid., Vol. V, *Ḥadīth* 561, p. 393.

13. Ibid.

14. 'Alī ؓ was the Prophet's ﷺ first cousin of Banū Hāshim of the Quraysh. He was the first minor (at the age of 12, some say 10) to accept Islam. He is one of the 10 who were given the glad tidings of Paradise on earth (*al-'Ashara al-Mubashsharīn*). It is he who was left in the Prophet's ﷺ bed when the Prophet ﷺ made *Hijra* (migrated) to Madina. He also became the son-in-law of the Prophet ﷺ after his marriage to his daughter Fāṭima. He had a fantastic memory and had memorised the Qur'ān in the Prophet's lifetime; he also related 586 *aḥādīth* from the Prophet ﷺ. He became the Fourth Rightly-Guided Caliph of Islam and was martyred in 40.

15. Ṭabarī, 'Tā'rīkh al-Ṭabarī', *The History of al-Ṭabarī*, Vol IX, 'The Last Years of the Prophet'. Trans. Ismail K. Poonawala. (Albany, State Uni. of New York, 1990), p. 51.

16. His full name is Aḥmad ibn Yaḥyā ibn Jābir ibn Dāwūd al-Balādhurī al-Baghdādī [from Baghdad] al-Kātib [the writer]. Some scholars think he was of Persian descent and his family worked for the 'Abbāsid government. He travelled widely but spent most of his life in Baghdad with his Shuyūkh. He did not write many books but the few he wrote were granted great status, as masters in the field. He wrote, *Ansāb al-Ashrāf, Futūḥ al-Buldān, Kitāb al-Buldān al-Kabīr*. Some of his students became great *'Ulamā'* of the time, including Muḥammad ibn al-Nadīm, Aḥmad ibn 'Amār, Abū Yūsuf Ya'qūb ibn Nu'aym, Wakī' al-Qāḍī.

17. *The History of al-Ṭabarī*, op. cit., Vol. IX, p. 52.

18. The Prophet of Allah's prophecy was fulfilled – Abū Dharr ؓ was staying at a village called al-Rabadha, about three day's journey from Madina on the way to Makka. There was no one with him except his wife and a worker. Abū Dharr had instructed that, on his death, they should wash him, wrap him in a shroud, and lay him on the open road. Inform the first caravan that passed by that he was Abū Dharr, a Companion of the Messenger of Allah, and that they should help them bury him. When he died (during 'Uthmān's Caliphate) they did as they were told and put his body on the open road. 'Abdullāh b. Mas'ūd (a Companion) had been approaching that place with a group of men from Iraq. They noticed the bier on the road, the camels nearly treading on it. Abū Dharr's worker went to them and said, 'This is Abū Dharr, the Messenger of Allah's Companion. Help us

to bury him.' ʿAbdullāh b. Masʿūd broke into tears, saying, 'The Messenger of Allah spoke the truth. You will walk alone, die alone, and be raised alone'. Then he and his companions got down and buried him, and ʿAbdullāh b. Masʿūd told them Abū Dharr's story.

19. See Qur'ān 7:73-79; 11:61-68; 25:38; 26:141-159; 27:45-53; 29:38; 41:17; 51:43-45; 54:23-31; 69:4-8; 85:9-14; 91:11-15.
20. Bukhārī, op. cit., Vol. V, *Ḥadīth* 703.
21. Imām Mālik in his *al-Muwaṭṭa'* states, 'The *sunna* is that there is no *jizya* due from women or children of People of the Book, and that *jizya* is only taken from men who have reached puberty. The people of *dhimma* and the magians do not have to pay any *zakāh* on their palms or their vines or their crops or their livestock. This is because *zakāh* is enjoined on the Muslims to purify them and to be given back to their poor, whereas *jizya* is levied on the People of the Book to humble them. As long as they are in the country they have agreed to live in, they do not have to pay anything on their property except the *jizya*. If, however, they trade in Muslim countries, coming and going in them, a tenth is taken from what they invest in such trade. This is because *jizya* is only imposed on them on conditions, which they have agreed on, namely that they will remain in their own countries, and that war will be waged for them on any enemy of theirs, and that if they then leave that land to go anywhere else to do business they will have to pay a tenth. Whoever among them does business with the people of Egypt, and then goes to Syria, and then does business with the people of Syria and then goes to Iraq and does business with them and then goes on to Madina, or Yemen, or other similar places, has to pay a tenth.

    'People of the Book and magians do not have to pay any *zakāh* on any of their property, livestock, produce or crops. The *sunna* still continues like that. They remain in the *dīn* they were in, and they continue to do what they used to do. If in any one year they frequently come and go in Muslim countries then they have to pay a tenth every time they do so, since that is outside what they have agreed upon, and not one of the conditions stipulated for them. This is what I have seen the people of knowledge of our city doing.'
22. Haykal, op. cit., p. 449.
23. Duma was an oasis town between Madyan and Damascus linking central Arabia and the mountains of al-Sham.
24. Ibn Isḥāq states the robe was stripped from Ukaydir. Al-Ṭabarī states it belonged to Ukaydir's brother Ḥasan.
25. Saʿd b. Muʿādh passed away as a result of injuries during the siege of Madina in 5AH.
26. Transmitted by both Bukhārī and Muslim – *Mishkāt*, Vol. II, p. 1365.

27. Abū Dāwūd transmits on the authority of Anas that the Messenger of Allah spared Ukaydir's life and made peace with him on the condition that he should pay *jizya*.
28. Bukhārī, op. cit.,Vol.V, *Ḥadīth* 702.
29. '...When I heard that the Prophet of Allah ﷺ was on his way back to Madina, I got deep in my concern, and began to think of false excuses, saying to myself, "How can I avoid his anger tomorrow?" And I took the advice of wise members of my family. When it was said that Allah's Prophet ﷺ had come near, all the evil false excuses vanished from my mind and I knew well that I could never come out of this problem by forging a false statement. Then I decided firmly to speak the truth. ...So when I came to Allah's Prophet ﷺ I greeted him. He smiled a smile of an angry person and then said, "Come on." So I came walking till I sat before him. He said to me, "What stopped you from joining us. Had you not purchased an animal for carrying you?" I answered, "Yes, O Allah's Prophet, but by Allah, if I were sitting before any person from among the people of the world other than you, I would have avoided his anger with an excuse...if today I tell a lie to seek your favour, Allah would surely make you angry with me in the near future. But if I tell you the truth, though you will get angry because of it, I hope for Allah's forgiveness. Really, by Allah, there was no excuse for me." Ka'b continues:

    'Then I remained in that state (i.e. without my wife) for ten more nights after that till my period of fifty nights was completed starting from the time when Allah's Prophet ﷺ prohibited the people from talking to us. When I had offered my *Fajr* (morning, dawn) prayers on the fifth morning on the rooftop of my house, and while I was sitting in the condition which Allah describes in the Qur'ān (i.e. my very soul seemed straitened to me and even the earth seemed narrow to me for all its spaciousness), I heard the voice of one who had ascended the mountain of Sala' calling with his loudest voice. "Ka'b ibn Mālik! Be happy, by receiving good tidings." I fell down in prostration before Allah, realising that relief has come.'
30. Ibn Isḥāq, op. cit., p. 678.
31. Bukhārī, Vol. 5, *Ḥadīth* 745, p. 529.
32. The *Muhājirūn* – those Muslims who migrated from Makka to Madina prior to the liberation of Makka in 8.
33. *Al-Anṣār* – 'The Helpers' – the term is used for the Muslim converts of Madina, who welcomed the Makkan migrants.
34. The Prophet's ﷺ Mosque adjoined his house and one could enter the house through the Mosque.
35. 'Ā'isha was Abū Bakr's daughter and wife of the Prophet ﷺ.
36. Paraphrased from the Qur'ān, *Āl 'Imrān* 3: 144.

37. Khan, Dr. Majid Ali, *The Pious Caliphs* (Kuwait, 1978).
38. Abdur Raḥmān ibn ʿAwf was one of the earliest converts to Islam. He made the *Hijra* to Ethiopia and was one of the ten given glad tidings of Paradise (*al-ʿAshara al-Mubashsharīn*). In Madina he became a famous businessman. He prospered in his business and with it his hand of charity extended further and further meeting the needs of poor Muslims and paying the expenses of the Muslim forces.
39. An Anṣārī who accepted Islam before the Prophet's ﷺ *Hijra*. He was instrumental in the pledge of ʿAqaba, where the *Anṣār* promised security and support to the Prophet ﷺ. He spent a great deal of time with the Prophet ﷺ and had committed the Qur'ān to memory in the Prophet's lifetime. He was the most knowledgeable in the affairs of *ḥarām* and *ḥalāl*. For his understanding of Islam he was appointed a teacher to the Makkans after they were liberated. He was also sent to Yemen for the same purpose and later by ʿUmar ؓ to al-Sham, where he died.
40. Another Anṣārī. He accepted Islam at the pledge of ʿAqaba. He was steadfast in Islam and eloquent in the recitation of the Qur'ān. He remained in Madina devoted to the service of Islam until he passed away in 29.
41. Zayd was a dedicated young intellectual who mastered the Hebrew and Syriac languages. He thus became one of the scribes of the noble Prophet ﷺ. On numerous occasions he was summoned to write down the revealed verses of the Qur'ān. During the Caliphate of Abū Bakr ؓ and ʿUmar ؓ it was Zayd ؓ who was appointed to supervise the compiling of the Qur'ān into a single volume.
42. Maulānā Muḥammad Yūsuf Kāndhlawī, op. cit., p. 559.
43. Ibid.
44. Letters of Haḍrat Abū Bakr Ṣiddīq, trans. Dr. M. Adil (Pakistan, 1984), p. 60.
45. ʿIkrima ibn Abī Jahl was the son of the most irreconcilable opponent of Islam and he himself remained an opponent of the faith until after the conquest of Makka in 8. The Messenger of Allah ﷺ upon the liberation of Makka granted a general pardon and amnesty to whoever entered the sacred mosque or Abū Sufyān's home. However he refused to grant amnesty to a few individuals, one of them being ʿIkrima. He ﷺ gave orders that they should be killed even if they were found under the covering of the Kaʿba. When ʿIkrima learnt of this, he fled. However, his wife Umm Ḥakīm appealed to the Messenger of Allah ﷺ. She said: 'O Messenger of Allah, ʿIkrima has fled from you to Yemen out of fear that you will kill him. Grant him security and Allah will grant you security.' 'He is secure,' promised the Merciful Prophet ﷺ. After ʿIkrima's conversion to Islam his valour and energies were devoted to its service. He played a pivotal role in quelling the *Ridda* rebellions. He passed away fighting at the battle of Ajnadayn (al-Ṭabarī), some say at the battle of Yarmuk. When the battle

was over, among the many martyred and wounded were the bodies of three wounded *mujāhidīn* – al-Ḥārith ibn Hishām, Ayyāsh ibn Abī Rabī'ah and 'Ikrima. Al-Ḥārith called for water to drink. As it was brought to him he noticed Ayyāsh's predicament and requested that it be given first to Ayyāsh. By the time they got to Ayyāsh, he had just breathed his last. When they turned to al-Ḥārith and 'Ikrima they found that they too had passed away. (Abdulwahid Hamid, *Companions of the Prophet*, MELS, London, 1985, Vol. I, p. 68.)

46. Letters of Haḍrat Abū Bakr, op. cit.

47. Maulānā Muḥammad Yūsuf Kāndhlawī, op. cit., p. 564.

48. He was a Qurayshī and at first an opponent of the Muslims. He accepted Islam after Hudaybiya and became one of its leading generals. Beside battles in al-Sham, he is credited with the liberation of Egypt, where he died in 43.

49. Yazīd was the son of the famous Qurayshī antagonist Abū Sufyān. Yazīd accepted Islam in 8 and championed the cause of Islam. After the death of Abū 'Ubayda ⚜, 'Umar ⚜ appointed him governor of al-Sham, a post he held for a brief period until his death in 18.

50. A Qurayshī and early convert to Islam. He fought alongside the Prophet ﷺ in Uḥud until the end. His sincerity and conviction were exemplary. He played a pivotal role in the election of Abū Bakr ⚜ to the *Khilāfa*. He passed away in the famous plague of Amwās in Palestine in 18. His epitaph cannot be surpassed by 'Umar's ⚜ statement, 'If Abū 'Ubayda ⚜ were alive, I would have nominated him to the *Khilāfa*.'

51. It is not certain whether Shuraḥbīl was a Qurayshī. However, he was certainly associated with them from very early on. He accepted Islam during the early period and he died in al-Sham around 18.

52. *The History of al-Ṭabarī*, op. cit., Vol. XI, p. 80.

53. al-Ṭabarī's full name is Abū Ja'far Muḥammad ibn Jarīr al-Ṭabarī (224-310/839-923). He memorized the Qur'ān by the age of seven and started writing down *aḥādīth* by the age of nine. He met many great '*Ulamā*' and studied under Imām Shāfi'ī and he learned *Qirā'āt* from Imām Aḥmad ibn Yūsuf al-Taqlabīy. His most famous book, *The History of Prophets and Kings* (*Tā'rīkh al-rusul wal-mulūk*) is an essential reference for any student of Islamic history. (Recently the State University of New York has published its English translation in 39 volumes.)

54. Hamidullah, Muhammad, *The Muslim Conduct of State* (Lahore, Sh. Muhammad Ashraf, 1942), p. 306.

3

The Confrontation

As a general guide the following dates are central to this study. Heraclius defeated the Persians in 7/628, the Battle of Mu'ta took place in 8/629 and, a few months later in early 9/630, Heraclius celebrated in Jerusalem by personally returning the relics of the 'True Cross'. Heraclius was still in al-Sham when the Prophet Muḥammad ﷺ undertook the expedition to Tabūk in 9/630. It is important to note that during this expedition the Prophet ﷺ made treaties with the Bishop of Ayla (ʿAqaba), the people of Jarbā, the people of ʿAdhura, and the local leader of Maʿān.[1]

The first encounter with the Byzantines, in the region of al-Balqa', was settled with signing of the peace treaty of Ma'ab. The first conflict with the Byzantines took place in 13/late 633 or early 634 when the Muslims attacked a small village of Gaza, called Dāthin. Thereafter, the commanders were engaged in various battles in different places at possibly the same time. This is one of the reasons why it is difficult to reconstruct the order of events. The general consensus among historians is that after Dāthin the first major battle was at Ajnadayn probably about the middle of 634. Around the same time the occupation of Damascus was taking place under the leadership of Abū ʿUbayda. Abū Bakr passed away on Tuesday 21 Jumādā al-Ākhira 13/22 August 634. The main battles that began during Abū Bakr's Caliphate and concluded in that of ʿUmar are the first occupation of Damascus in Rajab 14/635 and Ḥimṣ. The Muslims, however, evacuated Ḥimṣ and Damascus sometime before 636 in the face of a Byzantine counter-attack led by Theodore, brother of Heraclius and Vahan. Perhaps the most decisive battle in the liberation of al-Sham, the Battle of Yarmuk, took place in 15/20 August 636. After winning decisively on the banks of the river Yarmuk and expelling the Byzantine forces from the greater part of al-Sham, amidst much jubilation the Muslims were welcomed back as a liberating army into Ḥimṣ, Damascus and other major cities.

Also in 15/late 636 early 637, the peace treaty of al-Quds (Jerusalem) was signed by ʿUmar ibn al-Khaṭṭāb. Other cities to fall in Palestine in 15 included Gaza, Minas, Qinnaṣrīn and Caesarea. After Jerusalem the northern frontiers were subdued by ʿIyāḍ ibn Ghanam who, according to Balādhurī, was responsible for conquering the whole of Mesopotamia. Similarly, Egypt and the adjacent territory of northern Africa were conquered by ʿAmr ibn al-ʿĀṣ, who also set out in 15. The conquest of Egypt was finalized by 20/640-641 and in the same year on 11 February 641 Heraclius died. [*see* Map 4]

COURSE OF EVENTS IN AL-SHAM

After Abū Bakr's initiation of the Syrian expedition and appointment of the four commanders, there is insufficient evidence to name one as the supreme commander.[2] We can say with confidence that ʿAmr ibn al-ʿĀṣ[3] was the commander in the area of Palestine, Shuraḥbīl ibn Ḥasana in

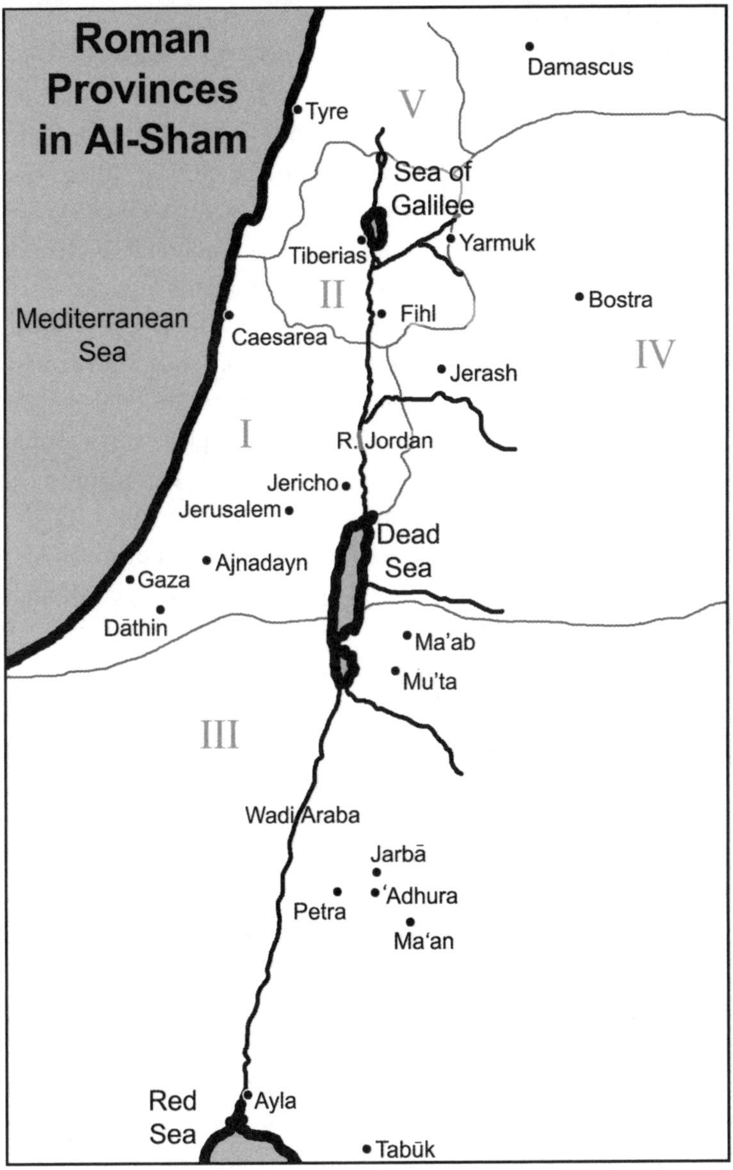

Map 4: Roman Provinces in al-Sham

the fertile middle Ḥūrān and Abū ʿUbayda ibn Jarraḥ ❀
around Damascus.

There has been an attempt to discredit the reliability of the
early Islamic historians on the ground that some state that
ʿAmr ibn al-ʿĀṣ ❀ was in charge, while others say it was Abū
ʿUbayda ❀ and still others Yazīd ibn Abū Sufyān. There is a
simple explanation for this apparent inconsistency. What
happened, and all historians are unanimous about it, is that, as
explained above, a zone of operation was designated for each
commander. When an engagement involved the forces of more
than one commander, the overall command was assumed by
the commander in whose zone of operation the engagement
was taking place. Thus, if a battle was taking place in Palestine,
ʿAmr ibn al-ʿĀṣ ❀ would assume the overall command even
though Yazīd ibn Abū Sufyān might be assisting him. In the
case of the battle of Damascus the chief commander was Abū
ʿUbayda ❀, because it was his zone of operation, even though
the other generals helped him.

Initially the Muslims moved with great caution and only
engaged themselves in giving *daʿwa* to the Arabic-speaking
populace of al-Sham. They also restricted themselves to the
open countryside rather than engage in battles with the
Byzantines in the fortified walled cities. The first general to be
involved with the Byzantines was Abū ʿUbayda ❀ who, on his
way to al-Sham, confronted the people of al-Balqāʾ. They put
up some resistance at first but sued for peace soon afterwards.
Accordingly, the first confrontation was resolved peacefully and
the peace agreement of Maʾāb was signed. The first conflict with
the Byzantines, which was led by ʿAmr ❀, took place at Dāthin,
a village in Gaza, near the residence of a Byzantine general. The
Muslim forces were victorious in this battle but they had
evidently alerted the Byzantines for a concerted effort. When
Heraclius was informed of the Muslim advance, he mustered a
large army and sent it out to check the Muslims. He sent his

brother Theodore with 90,000 men against ʿAmr ﵁. He also sent Jurjah ibn Tawdhura against Yazīd ﵁, and al-Duraqis against Shuraḥbīl ibn Ḥasana ﵁. He sent 60,000 men under the command of al-Fiqār ibn Naṣṭūs against Abū ʿUbayda ﵁.

The commanders became anxious and concerned at the overwhelming numbers of the Byzantine forces and began to express their fears to each other. ʿAmr ﵁ urgently despatched a courier to Abū Bakr ﵁ expressing his concerns and reporting the great numbers of the enemy, their superior armaments and sought advice on the course of action to be taken. On receipt of the letter, Abū Bakr ﵁ despatched a note to ʿAmr ﵁ asking him to join forces with the rest of the commanders. An often quoted letter attributed to Abū Bakr ﵁, is cited below. However the authenticity of this letter has not been established:

> Combine, so that you may be one army. Meet the armies of the polytheists with the army of the Muslims, for you are Allah's helpers. Allah comes to the aid of those who support Him and deserts those who show ingratitude to Him. The likes of you will not be destroyed on account of your small numbers. Rather, ten thousand will be destroyed if they were attacked from the rear. Therefore, take precautions about the rear. Join together at Yarmuk under your separate banners. Let every man among you unite with his companions.

Another note was despatched to Khālid ibn al-Walīd ﵁, who at the time was campaigning in Iraq, to head towards al-Sham with the greatest possible speed and offer assistance in al-Sham.

KHĀLID MOVES FROM IRAQ TO AL-SHAM

Upon receiving Abū Bakr's ﵁ letter in al-Ḥīra, Iraq, Khālid ibn al-Walīd ﵁ moved to al-Sham, leaving in command al-Muthannā ibn Ḥāritha al-Shaybānī. He assembled a force of some 500 to 800[4] men and prepared them for the journey to join their fellow Muslims in al-Sham. The precarious situation of Muslims in al-Sham as indicated by Abū Bakr's orders, required a speedy, direct march to reinforce them. After leaving al-Ḥīra, Khālid ؓ arrived at a place called Quraqir. From there he considered crossing the desert to save precious time. The proposed route would entail an arduous trek requiring six days (five nights) over terrain devoid of tracks or known watering holes. All the guides advised against such an expedition since no group of people or army had ever attempted such a feat before. But Khālid ؓ was adamant and convinced a renowned guide, Rāfiʿ ibn ʿUmayr al-Ṭā'ī to accompany them. Thereafter Khālid ؓ gave a sermon to the troops and reminded them: 'Do not by any means let your ways be diverse, nor your certainty weakened! Know that aid comes according to the level of the intention and reward according to the level of the good deed.'[5] This march across the uncharted desert in the burning heat must be ranked among the greatest military endurance achievements of all time.

The troops' valour was rekindled when they saw Khālid's enthusiasm and resolve. Khālid ؓ instructed them to give as much water to the camels as possible. Then they muzzled them and brought them along unloaded so as to reduce their consumption of water. The water they carried in large leather skins was soon used up. At this point, they slew the camels one by one[6] and extracted the water from their bellies, which they and the horses drank.

According to al-Ṭabarī: 'When he reached Suwāʿ and feared that the heat of the sun would overcome them, Khālid ؓ called Rāfiʿ: "What news do you have?" He answered, "Good. You have attained a copious source, for you are upon water." He urged them on, though he was perplexed and bleary eyed. He continued: "O people, look for two peaks that look like a

pair of female breasts, then come to them." When they spotted
them, they said, "Two peaks." He went up on them both and
said, "Dig to the right and to the left for a box-thorn (a low,
round shrub) like the seat of a man." They found its root and
said: "A root but we do not see any tree." He said, "Dig
wherever you will." They stirred up the dust to find small
quantities of water and swampy ground with sweet water
under the sand.'

For this gallant effort a poet wrote:

> How wonderful has Rāfiʿ been
> who succeeded in finding the way from Quraqir to Suwāʿ
> to the water from which the coward who attempts to
> reach it returns before attaining it.
> No human being before thee ever did that!

Thereafter, Khālid ⁂ attacked the village of Suwāʿ. One
description of that encounter should be treated with some
scepticism, given the Islamic teachings and general conduct as
dictated by Abū Bakr ⁂ to the army. It is reported that some
of the inhabitants were drinking wine around a large vat and a
singer was singing:

> Will you two not give me another drink before the army
> of Abū Bakr?
> Perhaps our deaths are near, though we do not know.[7]

Khālid ⁂ attacked and killed the singer, named Hurkus
according to Balādhurī, whose blood flowed into the vase from
which they were drinking. Thereafter Khālid ⁂ and his force
proceeded towards Marj Rāhiṭ.

At Marj Rāhiṭ he confronted the Banū Ghassānid while
they were celebrating the Easter festival (24 April 634/19 Ṣafar
13). He took much booty and many captives. From there he
travelled to Buṣrā (also known as Bostra or Qanāt Buṣrā), which

became the first city of al-Sham to be liberated from the Byzantine occupation and brought under Islamic rule.

With the exception of al-Ṭabarī[8] most Muslim historians including al-Wāqidī, Ibn Isḥāq, Balādhurī and Ibn Khaldūn confirm Khālid's emergence at or near Damascus. According to al-Ṭabarī, he emerged at Yarmuk. We can confirm that Khālid's point of departure was al-Ḥīra in Iraq but we need to make a choice on whether to accept al-Ṭabarī's report or the others on the point of emergence. Understanding Khālid's route will assist us in resolving the chronological problem concerning the first phase of the encounter.

THE ROUTE OF KHĀLID'S MARCH

Topographically, both Damascus and Yarmuk are equally likely places. However, if the chronology of events and the terrain that the Muslim armies were crossing from Madina are taken into account, it can be deduced that the battle of Ajnadayn in Palestine, which is nearer Madina, must have taken place first before the decisive encounter of Yarmuk. Also, consideration must be given to Abū Bakr's military tactics for he was totally against rapid advancement into enemy territory while exposing the rear. If the army did advance as far north as Yarmuk, then any potential retreat to Madina was cut off. Further, the Muslim armies' advance to Yarmuk before Ajnadayn would mean the Byzantine military posts of Palestine would have remained unchecked. There is also a chronological aspect. Khālid ﷺ arrived in al-Sham in April 634 and Abū Bakr ﷺ passed away on 22 August 634 (Tuesday 21 Jumādā al-Ākhira 13), while the Battle of Yarmuk was still in progress (according to al-Ṭabarī). One then needs to assume that for the four months between April and August, there were no major engagements on the Syrian front between the two

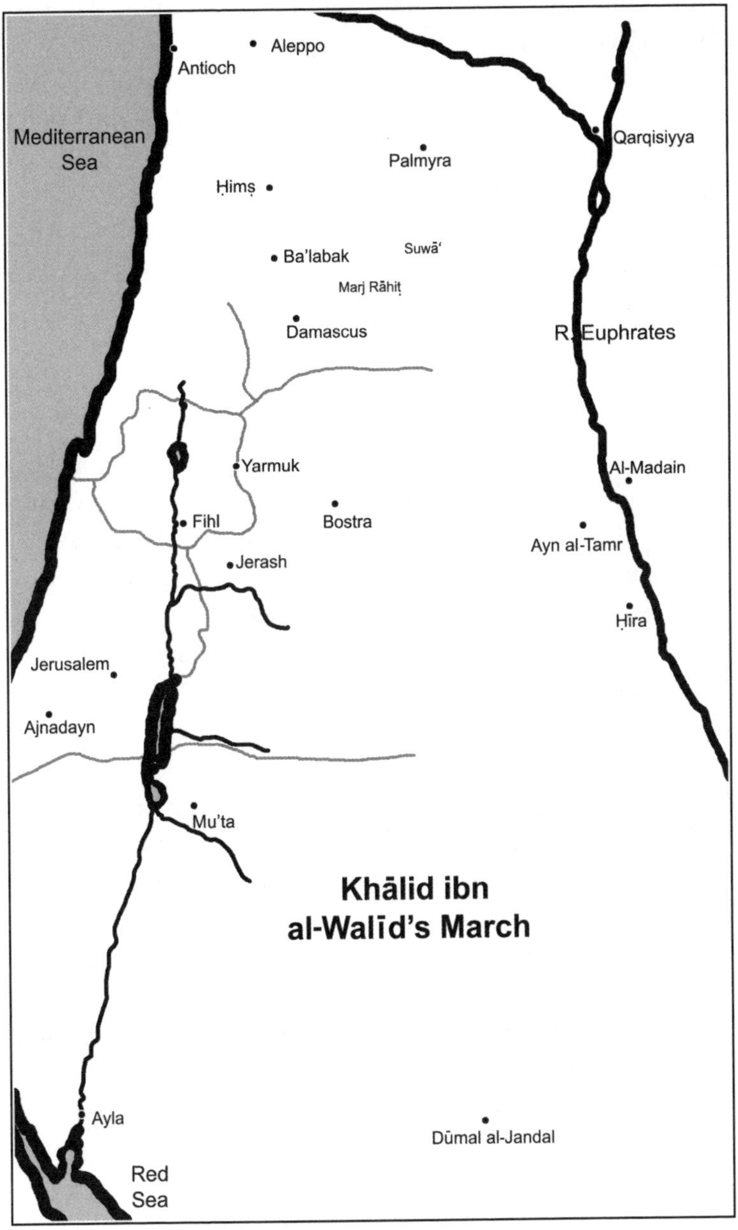

Map 5: Khālid's March

armies, but only preparations for the forthcoming Battle of Yarmuk. [*see* Map 5]

First, the majority of scholars are agreed that Khālid ؓ after having left al-Ḥīra, arrived at a place called Quraqir.[9] From here, Khālid ؓ with the assistance of Rāfiʿ ibn ʿUmār al-Ṭā'ī crossed waterless desert requiring a journey of six days (five nights) and emerged at the watering hole of Suwāʿ Thereafter he confronted the Banū Ghassānid at Marj Rāhiṭ, near Damascus while they were celebrating the Easter festival of the year 634[10] (around April 24/Ṣafar 13).

After having examined the classical sources only two routes taken by Khālid ؓ can be regarded as probable:

First, he took the shortest and quickest route from al-Ḥīra to Damascus by travelling northwest along the Euphrates towards Palmyra, crossing the desert at or near Qarqīsyā' after having passed ʿAyn al-Tamr. On route, according to al-Ṭabarī, he engaged in battle at Sandawada, al-Musayyakh, and raided the people of Suwāʿ. Then he made a peace agreement with the people of Arāk (25 km from Palmyra) and Palmyra. Further confrontations followed in al-Qaryatayy (midway between Palmyra and Damascus), Huwwārīn, Qusam and Marj Rāhiṭ. Ibn Isḥāq records that after ʿAyn al-Tamr he crossed the desert at Quraqir arriving at Suwāʿ where he confronted its people before arriving at Marj Rāhiṭ. This account is in agreement with al-Wāqidī.

Second, Khālid ؓ travelled southwest of al-Ḥīra towards Dūmat al-Jandal, where he engaged in battle and won. Thereafter he travelled to Kusam, where a peace agreement was signed, before advancing towards Palmyra by crossing the desert on a six-day journey. This is confirmed by Balādhurī.

All reports concur with Khālid's activities in Palmyra and Marj Rāhiṭ including that of Balādhurī who reports Khālid ؓ as first travelling southwest before taking a route northwest.

Balādhurī's report of Khālid's activities in Dūmat al-Jandal can be argued to have been misplaced because it is unlikely that Khālid ﵁ would have travelled south first before turning northwest when the command of urgency was ordered by Abū Bakr ﵁. With scrutiny it might be fair to assume that Balādhurī confused Khālid's activities in Dūmat al-Jandal at the time of his march with his very much earlier military gains while on his way to Iraq.

A final analysis of Khālid's exploits remains. There are four pieces of evidence to contend with.

First, almost all reports agree that Khālid ﵁ arrived at Marj Rāhiṭ and attacked the Ghassānids as they were celebrating their Easter, this being Ṣafar 13/23 April 634.

Second, al-Ṭabarī gives the date of Khālid's departure from al-Ḥīra in Iraq as Rabīʿ al-Ākhir 13 AH (June/July 634).

Third, once more there is concurrence among most of the other sources that Khālid ﵁ departed from al-Ḥīra after the *Ḥajj* of 12 AH (January/February 634).

It is a fact that early historians were very particular about festive days and therefore both the mention of Easter and *Ḥajj* need very serious consideration in evaluating the chronology. From the evidence it is obvious that al-Ṭabarī's reporting on the authority of Sayf, stating Khālid ﵁ to have arrived at Marj Rāhiṭ (in Ṣafar, i.e. April) before his departure (in Rabīʿ al-Ākhir, i.e. June/July) is impossible and therefore inadmissible. This leaves us with the option that he departed from al-Ḥīra immediately after the *Ḥajj* of 12, which was early February. There is one further point to consider.

Fourth, according to Balādhurī, Abū Bakr ﵁ despatched the troops for al-Sham from Madina in Ṣafar 13 (March/April 634). This again brings chronological problems for it seems impossible for the troops to have travelled deep enough into al-Sham, assessed the Byzantine armies, requested help from Abū Bakr ﵁ and for Abū Bakr ﵁ to have despatched a courier to Khālid 🌼 so that he would arrive in Marj Rāhiṭ in late April.

In order to solve this problem we need to revert to Balādhurī who mentions the troops were ready and stationed at Jurf before Muḥarram (February/March 634). It is, therefore, possible that the troops began to leave Madina before the stated date by Balādhurī and that only the last battalion of the first wave departed in Ṣafar. On this hypothesis, the chronology becomes much more plausible for it allows Abū Bakr 🌼 to have despatched the first wave of forces of 'Amr ibn al-'Āṣ 🌼 in January/February 634. This would have given them enough time to traverse the southern plains of al-Sham and request reinforcements from Madina in late March or even early April 634, then for Abū Bakr 🌼 to instruct Khālid 🌼 who was at that time in Iraq. This would have allowed Khālid 🌼 enough time to receive orders from Madina, march across the desert for six days and appear in Marj Rāhiṭ near Damascus on the Easter of 634 (24 April 634).

Some accounts of Khālid's march as stated above mention several battles on his way to al-Sham. This is unlikely as his primary objective was to get to al-Sham as quickly as possible. This is not to say the battles credited to Khālid 🌼 did not take place, rather that they have been misplaced and confused with earlier or later engagements. In particular his campaign of Dūmat al-Jandal, which is to the south of his proposed shortest route and Jabal Bishr to the far north on the banks of the Euphrates.

BUṢRĀ (Bostra)

As stated earlier, after Khālid 🌼 had defeated the Ghassānids, he arrived at Buṣrā. Here, either before the battle or afterwards, he reunited with the other commanders in Syria,

Abū 'Ubayda ⬥, Yazīd ibn Abī Sufyān ⬥ and Shuraḥbīl ibn Ḥasana ⬥.

Buṣrā surrendered and, according to unconfirmed reports narrated by Balādhurī the inhabitants made terms agreeing to pay for each adult one dinar and one *jarīb* (specified measure) of wheat.

From here all four commanders seem to have moved towards Palestine to assist 'Amr ibn al-'Āṣ, who was confronting a large Byzantine army.

AJNADAYN

Ajnadayn, a strategic locality identified as being 25 kilometres west-southwest of Jerusalem[11] saw the first major battle between the Muslims and the Byzantine forces. Heraclius, having received news of the Muslim advance, mobilized a large force of about 90,000[12] under the command of his brother, Theodore.

The Muslims' commander was 'Amr ibn al-'Āṣ ⬥, while the other commanders gave him their full support. A fierce battle ensued and many casualties were recorded on both sides before the Byzantines' spirit finally wavered and they took flight. Khālid ⬥ in particular is reported to have shown great chivalry and Ṭulayb ⬥, who was the Prophet's ﷺ cousin (son of 'Urwa, the daughter of 'Abd al-Muṭṭalib), fought a duel with a Roman who severed his right hand making him drop his sword. Thereafter the Romans surrounded him and killed him. The Muslim martyrs reported by Balādhurī included: 'Abdullāh ibn az-Zubair ibn 'Abd al-Muṭṭalib ibn Hāshim, Ṭulayb ibn 'Umar, and 'Ikrima ibn Abī Jahl.

According to most accounts this battle took place in the last month[13] of Abū Bakr's Caliphate and the news of the Muslims' victory reached him while he was confined to bed in his final illness.

FIHL (Pella)[14]

After the defeat of the Byzantines at Ajnadayn, those who refused to sign the peace agreement and pay the *jizya* scattered further north and regrouped again in the region of eastern Jordan by the banks of the river Jordan.

The Muslim forces advanced to face the Byzantines who, on seeing the Muslims approach, destroyed the banks and dams of the river Jordan in order to flood the region, and so impede passage for the Muslims. As the Muslims approached, unaware of the Byzantine tactics, their horses became mired in the mud. After great difficulty, patience and endurance they traversed the hurdle and confronted them in Fihl.

After a prolonged battle in which many lost their lives – Balādhurī quotes a figure of one hundred thousand Byzantine casualties – they were defeated. Some Byzantine *rāfida*[15] fled to Damascus while others complied with the Muslim terms and preferred to pay the *jizya*.

While the Muslims were in the vicinity of Fihl, at a place called al-Yakusha[16] they were brought the devastating news of Abū Bakr's ❁ death. The news was kept from the forces until the victory of Fihl.

The Battle of Fihl was fought in Dhū al-Qa'da 13/27 December 634 to 25 January 635. Both Ibn Ishāq and Balādhurī give the specific date of 28 Dhū al-Qa'da 13. This is five months into 'Umar ibn al-Khaṭṭāb's Caliphate.

There is a vogue amongst certain authors with jaundiced views to accuse 'Umar ibn al-Khaṭṭāb ❁ of harbouring animosity towards Khālid ibn al-Walīd ❁. They assert that 'Umar ibn al-Khaṭṭāb ❁ removed Khālid ❁ from the command of the forces in Syria as soon as he was appointed Caliph, and furthermore, that his very first action was to despatch a letter to Abū 'Ubayda ❁ informing him of his wishes.

However, historical research shows that Khālid ﷺ was only requested to step down either during the siege of Damascus or the Battle of Yarmuk in Rajab 14 (August/September 635) and Rajab 15 respectively some twelve to twenty-four months into ʿUmar's Caliphate.

After Ajnadayn and Fihl the *rāfida* of the Byzantine army escaped to the safety of the strongly fortified city of Damascus. The Muslims followed them there and encamped outside its walls.

DAMASCUS

The Muslim generals took up position at the different gates of Damascus. According to Balādhurī, Khālid ibn al-Walīd ﷺ camped at the Eastern Gate (al-Bāb ash-Sharqī), ʿAmr ibn al-ʿĀṣ ﷺ was at the Bāb Tūma, Shuraḥbīl ibn Ḥasana ﷺ at the Paradise Gate (Farādīs Gate), Abū ʿUbayda ﷺ at the Jābiya Gate and Yazīd ibn Abī Sufyān ﷺ was to control the area from the Little Gate (Ṣaghīr Gate) to the Kaysān Gate. There was also a battalion stationed at Barza some five kilometres from Damascus on the route to Ḥimṣ, under the leadership of Abū al-Dardā' ﷺ and ʿUwaiymir ibn ʿĀmir al-Khazrajī ﷺ to block any Byzantine reinforcements approaching Damascus. According to Sayf, a further battalion under the leadership of al-Qamah ibn Ḥakīm ﷺ was despatched to be stationed between Damascus and Palestine.

The Byzantines in Damascus pinned their hopes on the severe winter and reinforcements from Heraclius, who was stationed in Ḥimṣ (some say Antioch), to deter the Muslims. However, the Muslims held their ground and resolve. As for the reinforcements Heraclius despatched, Abū al-Dardā' easily checked them.

The siege, according to al-Wāqidī,[17] lasted for six months. Sayf reported seventy days and Balādhurī four months. The

Byzantines lost their courage and lost their resolve proportionally with time, in stark contrast to the Muslims, whose zeal increased.

ENTRY INTO DAMASCUS

There are two main plausible accounts of the Muslims' entry into Damascus, which need analysing. All classical reports agree that while one commander was taking the city by force at one gate, the inhabitants rushed towards the opposite gate, renounced resistance and sued for peace. As to which commander – Khālid ﷺ or Abū ʿUbayda ﷺ – played which role, this cannot be ascertained with full confidence.

First, according to Balādhurī: one night a friend of the Bishop came out of the city to inform Khālid ﷺ that its inhabitants were celebrating a feast and the Eastern Gate (where Khālid ﷺ was stationed) was sparsely manned and blocked with stones only.

Khālid ﷺ grasped the opportunity. He ordered inflatable skins, which he used to float across the moat. Once against the wall, he procured a ladder, climbed the wall and taking onto the few guards by surprise overcame them. Then he swung open the gates.

All this took place just before sunrise. Meanwhile at the Jābiya Gate, Abū ʿUbayda ﷺ made a direct assault on the gate, which was on the brink of collapse.[18] This made the Byzantines rush towards the gates in order to defend them. After a prolonged battle, the Byzantines took flight. The Bishop realising the imminent collapse of the city, rushed towards the Eastern Gate where Khālid ﷺ had just descended and surrendered to him. The Bishop and Khālid ﷺ entered the heart of the city, with the Bishop carrying the text of the peace agreement written by Khālid ﷺ. Abū ʿUbayda ﷺ and Khālid ﷺ met at '*al-Maksala*' (the quarter of the coppersmiths).

Abū 'Ubayda ⬥ added his signature to the document, even though he had entered the city by assault, and the whole city was treated as having surrendered peacefully.

Second, al-Ṭabarī on Sayf's authority narrates: one night, after the birth of a child to the Patrikios' wife, who was in charge of the troops, a feast was held. Khālid ⬥ through his intelligence agents became aware of this and planned to cross the moat and force an entry. After swimming across the moat he climbed the wall at the most difficult point, where the Byzantines least expected an attack. From the top of the wall he called out his signal, which was the *takbīr*, to inform his troops to assault the gate. He then climbed down on the inside and overpowered the guards and opened the gates. The Byzantines were confused and in a state of frenzy. When they heard of Khālid's entry they rushed to the other gates and opened them, allowing the Muslims to enter peacefully.

The Muslim commanders met in the centre of the city, not knowing whether to consider the city as having fallen by force or peacefully. After deliberation they agreed to treat the whole city as a territory surrendered peacefully.[19]

The decision to consider the city as gained by peaceful means, was derived from the guiding principle, stated in the Qur'ān and the *Sunna* of the Prophet of Allah ⬥:

> But if they (the enemy) incline towards peace, incline towards peace and put your trust in Allah: for He is the One that hears and knows (all things). (al-Anfāl 8: 61)

The aim of the Muslim forces was to establish peace, not to annihilate the enemy. Above all their object was to proclaim the word of Allah, not to seek worldly gain.

The prejudiced critics, who assert that the Muslims only engaged in war to acquire booty and pillage towns must acknowledge the magnanimity shown by the Muslim forces in Damascus and learn from it.

> *And fight them until there is no more tumult or oppression and the religion is for Allah; but if they desist, let there be no hostility except to those who do evil.* (al-Baqara 2: 193)

In the preceding verse (*al-Baqara* 2: 192) the Muslims are reminded: 'But if they desist, Allah is Oft-forgiving, Most Merciful.' Here the Muslims are reminded of Allah's attributes and urged to shift their attitudes towards forgiveness and mercy when confronted with an enemy who surrenders.

The sincere soldiers of Islam forfeited their claim to booty and decided to consider Damascus as a city gained by peaceful terms. If their aim had been material gain, they were in a position to have considered Damascus as taken by force and so laid claim to the rich booty. However, the occupants of the city were not only spared their lives; their wealth and property, their farms, houses and churches were also left untouched.

At the outset, the *jizya* consisted of one *jarīb* of wheat and one dinar per head. However, ʿUmar ibn al-Khaṭṭāb ﷺ made it four dinars on those who possessed gold and forty dirhams on those who possessed silver, along with provisions for the Muslims and three days' hospitality.[20]

According to both Ibn Isḥāq and al-Wāqidī, the capture of Damascus occurred in Rajab 14 (21 August to 19 September 635). Balādhurī states that the date on the capitulation agreement is Rabīʿ al-Thānī 15. This is because when Khālid ﷺ drafted the original document no date was put on it. When the Muslims departed from Damascus in order to check the Byzantine forces in Yarmuk, the Bishop came to Khālid ﷺ asking him to renew the statement and add as witnesses the other commanders. Khālid ﷺ granted the request and inserted the names of Abū ʿUbayda ﷺ, Yazīd ibn Abī Sufyān ﷺ and

Shuraḥbīl ibn Ḥasana ﷺ as witnesses. The date he wrote was the one on which the statement was renewed.

ḤIMṢ (Emesa)

Ḥimṣ was one of the major cities in al-Sham, a centre of commerce and religious pilgrimage. There was a famous temple dedicated to the sun. After securing Damascus, one commander, according to Ibn Isḥāq, Yazīd ibn Abī Sufyān ﷺ, remained within the city and the others fanned out over the territory. Abū ʿUbayda ﷺ moved towards Ḥimṣ and, on the way, took Baʿlabak after a minor skirmish. Abū ʿUbayda ﷺ wrote the following agreement for them:

> In the name of Allah, the Compassionate, the Merciful. This is a statement of security to (names of individuals from Baʿlabak) – Greeks, Persians and Arabs – for their lives, possessions, churches and houses, inside and outside the city and also for their mills. The Greeks are entitled to give pasture to their cattle within a space of 15 miles, yet are not to abide in any inhabited town. After Rabīʿ al-Thānī and Jumādā al-Ūlā have passed, they are at liberty to go where they will. Whosoever of them adopts Islam, shall have the same rights as we and be bound by the same obligations, and their merchants are entitled to go whither they will in the countries that have become ours through capitulation. Those of them who do not adopt Islam are bound to pay *jizya* and *kharāj*. Allah is witness and His witness is sufficient.[21]

After Baʿlabak the generals encamped outside the walls of Ḥimṣ. The people of Ḥimṣ shut themselves behind the safety of their walls and trusted to the promise of reinforcements from Heraclius and the impending bitter winter to wear down the Muslims' resolve. They believed that a people whose staple diet was a little camel milk and meat would not survive the severe, cold conditions. Time proved otherwise as the winter seemed to have no effect on the Muslims' resolve. In fact the situation of the Byzantines worsened, it is even alleged that the feet of some of them fell off in their shoes. As for the Muslims, not even a toe of theirs was hurt, though they were wearing sandals.[22]

While the Muslims were encamped outside Ḥimṣ, they became aware of a large force advancing towards the city. This was the long-awaited reinforcement of Byzantine troops sent by Heraclius. Abū ʿUbayda ﷺ despatched a battalion to check them. When the Byzantines saw the Muslims advancing towards them they retreated. The Muslims gave chase. When the inhabitants of Ḥimṣ saw the retreat of their relief forces and the failure of winter to dampen the Muslims' determination, they held counsel and agreed to sue for peace.

Other small villages, including Ḥamā (Epiphania), Famiya, Shayzar (Larissa), az-Zarra, al-Qaṣṭal, Maʿarrat Ḥimṣ (Maʿarrat an-Nuʿmān) were also subdued during this phase. Balādhurī reports that the people of Shayzar and Maʿarrat Ḥimṣ came out in welcoming parties, playing tambourines and singing before the Muslim forces.

Ibn Isḥāq dates the conquest of Ḥimṣ in Dhū al-Qaʿda 14 (14 December 635 to 14 January 636).

YARMUK

The turning point of the Byzantine occupation of al-Sham came after the Battle of Yarmuk. This was undoubtedly the most violent encounter between the Muslims and Byzantines, resulting in the loss of tens of thousands of lives.

Paradoxically, it was the Byzantine military tactics that resulted in the climax of the battle at Yarmuk. Heraclius, who was stationed at Antioch and aware of the Muslim gains, drew on his military skills and planned to expel them from al-Sham. In order to achieve this he decided to amass a large military force from throughout his empire and converge at one place thereby forcing the Muslims out of the recently occupied cities to confront him.[23]

Initially the plan seemed to work. As the Muslim forces became aware of the Byzantine build up, they took counsel from Madina. They decided to withdraw from the cities, just as Heraclius had envisaged, and group together in order to concentrate their forces and be able to counter the mighty Byzantine army.

As for the inhabitants of the various cities who had now been under Muslim rule for the better part of a year, this was unwelcome news for memories of religious oppression and burdensome taxes under Byzantine rule were still fresh in their minds. As for the Muslims, before they vacated from the various cities that had surrendered and paid *jizya*, they refunded the tax in full apologising that they could no longer protect them since they had to fight to save Islam and themselves. When the people of Ḥimṣ were handed back their *jizya*, some began to weep, and said: 'We like your rule and justice far better than the state of oppression and tyranny in which we were. The army of Heraclius we shall indeed, with your help repulse from the city.'[24] The Jews, who had been severely persecuted and repeatedly massacred throughout Byzantine history said: 'We swear by the Torah, no governor of Heraclius shall enter the city of Ḥimṣ unless we are first vanquished and exhausted.' This reaction was not peculiar to Ḥimṣ, the same was repeated from city to city, including Damascus.[25] The expressions of appreciation for the new and just Muslim rulers are unequalled in history. [*see* Maps 6a, 6b and 6c]

Military Force

In addition to the regular Byzantine army, Heraclius collected forces from throughout al-Sham, Mesopotamia and Armenia. Significant numbers of Syrian Arabs were conscripted from the tribes of Lakhm, Judham, Balqayn, Balī, ʿĀmila, Quḍāʿa and Ghassānid. The Arabs were commanded by Jabala ibn al-Ayham al-Ghassānī, a king of the Ghassānid tribe. The Armenians were commanded by Jaraja (George or Gargis). Heraclius gave the supreme command[26] to a eunuch, al-Saqalar, and a Persian, General Bahan (Vahan).[27]

The Muslims were commanded by Abū ʿUbayda ﷺ and the other generals present provided full support. As there are no records left behind by the Roman historians, the size of their army has to be derived from the records left by Muslim historians. Unfortunately the figures reported by most of them are somewhat on the high side. However, all are agreed that the Muslims were outnumbered approximately four to one. If the combined forces despatched from Madina during the first wave was 24,000 and both Abū Bakr ﷺ and ʿUmar ﷺ continued to supply reinforcements, and Khālid ibn al-Walīd's small contingent from Iraq is also taken into account an estimate of Muslim forces put at just over 30,000 is justified. We can, therefore, deduce that the Byzantines had amassed nearly 100,000 fighters. This would then concur with Ibn Isḥāq's report.

Selection of Site

The Battle of Yarmuk was fought along the two tributaries of the river Yarmuk, Wādī Ruqqād and Wādī ʿAllān around the towns of Jābiya, Tal al-Jamuʿa, Yaqūsa and north of Adhirʿāt. This was not an accidental battle site but a place well contrived and calculated by Heraclius, into which the Muslims were lured.

The Byzantines had three main reasons for selecting this site:

1. They greatly valued the advice of Niketas, a close companion of Heraclius. He was the son of the famous Persian general Shahrbaraz, who had successfully commanded the Persian forces in 613-14, in which the Byzantines suffered a crushing defeat and in particular used the area around Yarmuk to inflict devastating blows on the Byzantines. Whether Niketas was present during these battles is not certain, but it is reasonable to assume that Niketas must have learnt a few military tactics from his father and, in particular, how to take advantage of the topography around Yarmuk. Niketas, whom Heraclius used in several battles in al-Sham, played a pivotal role in the selection of the site.

2. There were a sizeable proportion of Jews from the tribe of Banū Naḍīr, who had been expelled from Madina in 4, who had settled at Adhirʿāt. It is true that the Jews, who were persecuted throughout the Byzantine-occupied territories of al-Sham, had preferred to ally themselves with the Muslims. It was, therefore, prudent for Heraclius to avoid any area where the Jews might assist the Muslims. However, Heraclius was astute enough to realize that, while the large community of Jews around Adhirʿāt, a strategically positioned town near the river Yarmuk, were not his confederates, they nevertheless bore enough grudges against the Muslims for having expelled them from Madina, at least not to support or assist the Muslims.

3. The Banū Ghassānid tribe were the supreme allies of the Byzantine Empire and Yarmuk was their home territory, where their tribesmen pastured their flocks.[28] Further, it was paramount for them to have control of this area for the wealth that accrued from important trade routes and the rich fertile land. It was they who were to

> supply the bulk of the manpower, raw materials and food. It is they who had also participated in the battles against the Persians in 614, and their importance cannot be underestimated.

Unfortunately, there are no records relating to the Battle of Yarmuk from Byzantine historians. One can only assume that the event that meant the collapse of the Byzantine rule in al-Sham (later Egypt), and in particular the rule of Heraclius, was too painful to record, or that any records were destroyed.

Tactics

Having succeeded in drawing the Muslims out of the walled cities into the open, in favourable terrain, Heraclius must have anticipated success.

It is reasonable to assume the Byzantines must have employed the military tactics handed down by previous Roman generals in the *Strategikon*. Muslim scholars record that the Byzantines occupied the high ground around the Yarmuk tributaries. Their main camp was near Wādī Ḥarir, some distance from the place of battle to allow their cavalry enough room for manoeuvre.[29] Byzantine military strategists also recommended noise by way of drums and shouting and this was used thunderingly at Yarmuk. Delaying the main engagement was another tactic recommended by Roman military manuals. It is reported that the two armies faced each other for over four weeks before the actual battle commenced. This period was used by the Byzantines to receive further reinforcements, gather intelligence, try and impress upon the Muslims their superiority and, in particular, try to recruit defectors. In that the Byzantines failed miserably.

The stage was now set, for what proved to be, without doubt, the most decisive battle between the Byzantines and the

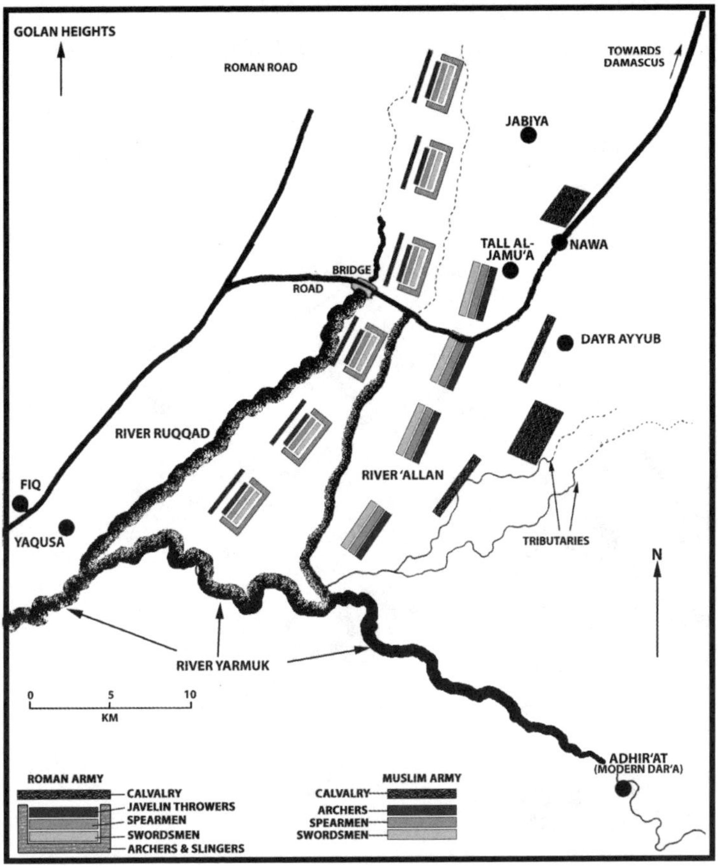

Map 6a: Muslim Army Assembly

Muslims. For the Muslims a loss here would have been an annihilation of not only the army but even the security of Madina. The future of Islam was at stake.

Confrontation

Before the fighting began it is likely that both sides tried to win over the forces of the other side. No records show of any Muslim defectors. According to Sayf in al-Ṭabarī, the Muslims

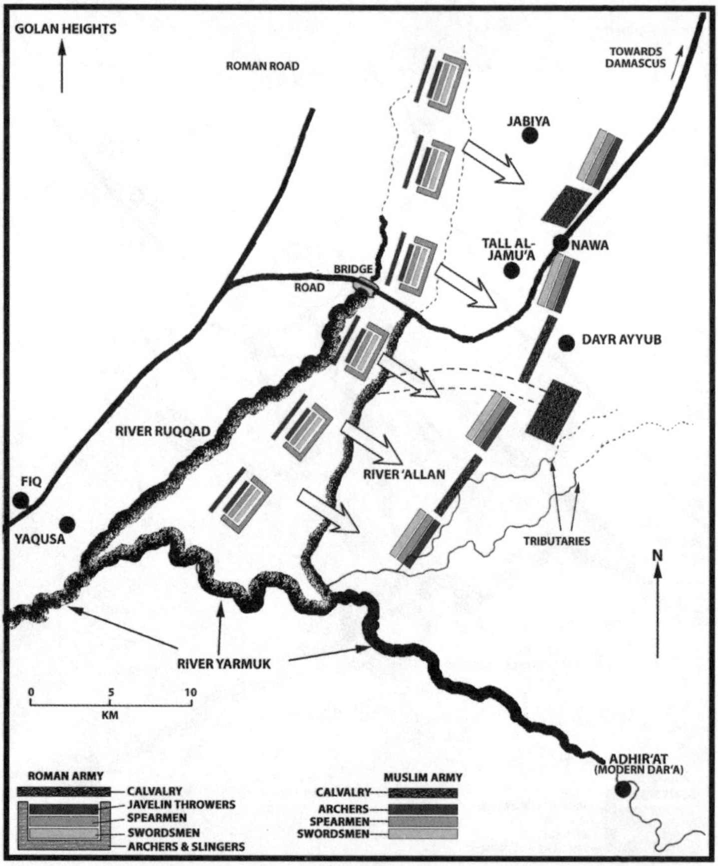

Map 6b: Attack of Roman Army

were called over for negotiations with the Byzantine command. They were welcomed to silk-covered pavilions, which the Muslims refused to enter. The Byzantines, rebuffed in this way had to come out to meet them. A carpet was rolled out, which the Muslims disdained. The two sides failed to reach an agreement. There are many reports on the dialogue between them but not supported with evidence. No doubt, the Muslims will have offered the Byzantines the normal terms of accepting Islam, paying the *jizya* or fighting. Stratos on the authority of

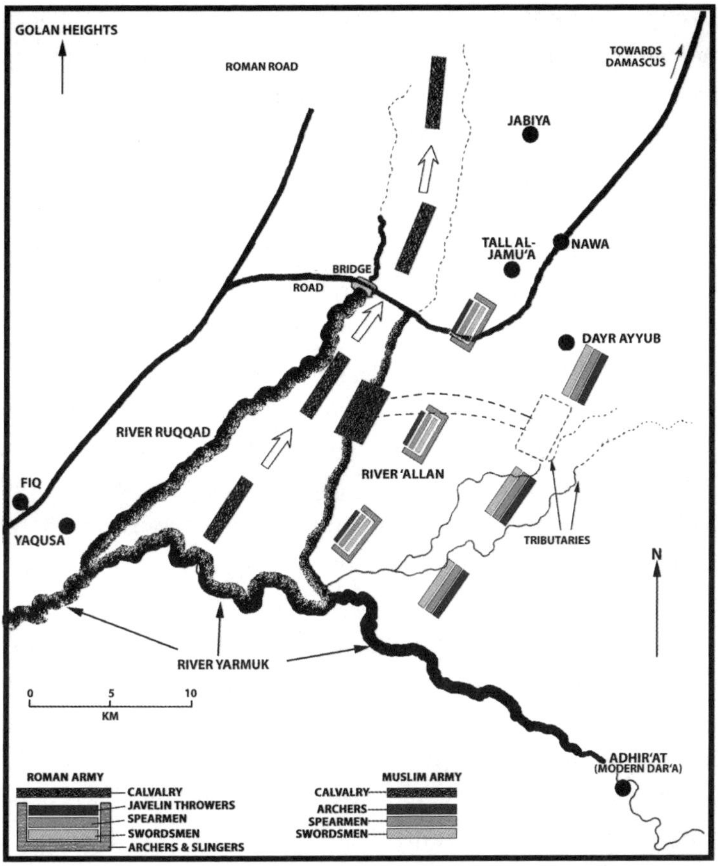

Map 6c: Attack of Muslim Army

Mirkhond relates: The Muslims were offered a payment of 10,000 gold coins for the Caliph ʿUmar ﵁, 5,000 to ʿUbayda ﵁ and Khālid ﵁, and 100,000 to be distributed among the forces, only to be rejected and requested to either embrace Islam or pay *jizya*. Having failed to reach a negotiated settlement the Muslims returned to prepare for battle.

The Byzantines arrayed their battalions; the infantry interlocked their shields and the horizon before the Muslims filled with heavily armed soldiers. Their priests, inciting revenge, arousing national passion and building confidence, marched in front of the soldiers with their crosses held high on poles. The Muslims under the command of Abū ʿUbayda[30] waited, with some, like Abū Sufyān, reciting verses from the Qur'ān to inspire and encourage the Muslim warriors.

Initially, single combats took place and the first Byzantine soldier was successfully defeated by Qays ibn Habīra. This was a good omen that lifted the spirits of the Muslims. However, soon after that a heavy Byzantine onslaught with cavalry and infantry pushed the Muslims back, throwing them into disarray and breaking their lines of defence. Many started retreating towards their camp. There many of the Muslims' ladies, observing the spectacle armed themselves with swords and took to the battlefield,[31] whilst others gave encouragement to their men urging them to face the enemy with resolve.

Khālid, who was positioned behind the infantry, made a lightning counter-attack with his cavalry and took the Byzantines by surprise. They retreated faster than they had advanced, their ranks broken. In the ensuing disorder, Khālid noticed a gap emerging between the Byzantine infantry and the cavalry and he occupied the middle ground thus dividing the Byzantine forces. The Byzantines were trapped with their right, left and rear flanks against the steep ravines of the river Yarmuk and its tributaries and the Muslims in front of them. The Muslims then opened up their ranks and made a gap, giving a welcome opportunity for many of the Byzantine cavalry to escape. With the cavalry in full flight the infantry was effectively stranded.

Many lost their lives on the battlefield but a greater number died trying to flee across the river Yarmuk. The muddy banks became a snare they could not escape. The river changed colour to that of human blood, as over half the Byzantine force that tried to escape via the river were claimed by it.

The battle was fought over several days and many Muslims also died[32] and as many were injured. Abū Sufyān[33] lost his eye when an arrow pierced it.

Balādhurī and Ibn Isḥāq state the battle took place in Rajab 15/15 August to 15 September 636.[34]

AFTER YARMUK

Some of the fleeing Byzantine army tried to find refuge in walled cities like Damascus and Ḥimṣ; others rushed to the Emperor in Antioch. Abū ʿUbayda ﷺ, leaving behind a commander at Yarmuk, gave chase and the cities of Ḥimṣ and Damascus were subdued for a second time. This time there was no significant resistance, as the local inhabitants had previously tasted the justice and dignity under Muslim rule.

Heraclius, in Antioch, lost hope after Yarmuk and became despondent. Although at this stage the greater part of al-Sham was still under Byzantine rule, morale and the will to resist had dissipated. Heraclius and his generals made their said adieux: 'Peace unto you, O Syria, what an excellent country this is for the enemy.'[35] With his family and comrades, sometime in late September 636, Heraclius made his way to Constantinople via Edesa.

A Greek authority, Michael the Syrian, states that before Heraclius departed he ordered his men to plunder the whole of the remaining area.

The overall command of al-Sham was now in the hands of Abū ʿUbayda ﷺ and he directed his generals to spread out and stabilize the country.

It is difficult to ascertain which of the generals, ʿAmr ibn al-ʿĀṣ ﷺ, Khālid ibn al-Walīd ﷺ, Yazīd ibn Abī Sufyān ﷺ, or Ziyād ibn Ḥanẓala ﷺ, were involved in subduing the various cities. One fact is nonetheless certain, they were all under the command of Abū ʿUbayda ﷺ. The chronology is also obscured as several commanders were in action at various places at the same time.

QINNAṢRĪN, ALEPPO AND ANTIOCH

In a very short period of time Qinnaṣrīn (Chalcis), Aleppo, al-Rawḥa, Caesarea, Baysān and Antioch came under Muslim control.

Minas, the Byzantine commander, possibly second in command to Heraclius, put up a feeble resistance at Qinnaṣrīn. The resistance proved disastrous, as most of the Byzantines including Minas lost their lives. Those in surrounding villages surrendered and were spared. Al-Ṭabarī credits[36] this to Khālid ﷺ and further states: 'When ʿUmar ﷺ heard of this in praise of Khālid ﷺ, ʿUmar ﷺ said: Khālid has made himself Amir! May Allah have mercy on Abū Bakr! He had better understanding of people than I have.'

Balādhurī reports that the inhabitants revolted after the generals had departed and broke the covenant. Abū ʿUbayda ﷺ directed a second general, Ṣimt ibn al-Aswad to the city. The treacherous were subdued and peace brought to the city once more.

The capture of Aleppo is credited to ʿIyāḍ ibn Ghanm al-Fihrī, who negotiated terms with its inhabitants. They were granted the safety of their lives, their possessions, city walls, churches, homes and the fort. With a small proviso for a piece of land to build a mosque, ʿIyāḍ agreed the terms and Abū ʿUbayda ﷺ later sanctioned them.[37]

Antioch initially offered some resistance, with its inhabitants locking themselves behind the gates of the walled city. The Muslims laid siege and the Byzantines surrendered. They were offered the option of paying the *jizya* or leaving. A few decided to evacuate and for them a safe passage was granted. Like the inhabitants of Aleppo, however, the Antiochians rebelled and broke the covenant. Abū ʿUbayda ﷺ despatched ʿIyāḍ ibn Ghanm and Ḥabīb ibn Maslama[38] who duly brought them under control once again.

The control of Antioch was a great psychological victory for the Muslims as the seat of Heraclius was now under their control. ʿUmar ﷺ requested Abū ʿUbayda ﷺ to station a strong Muslim garrison in the city. From here the generals converged upon the first *Qibla* (direction of prayer) of Islam, the second house of worship built on earth and the third holiest Mosque, al-Aqṣā in Jerusalem.

JERUSALEM

ʿAmr ibn al-ʿĀṣ ﷺ, whose territory was southern Palestine, returned to it after the Battle of Yarmuk and laid siege to Jerusalem. However, he was not successful in liberating Jerusalem. After his expedition in northern al-Sham was completed, Abū ʿUbayda ﷺ marched and joined forces with ʿAmr ﷺ near Jerusalem. The inhabitants of Jerusalem, which contained no Jews, applied for a conditional surrender and undertook to open the gates if the Caliph, ʿUmar ﷺ, came in person. The Muslims, could have ignored this condition and taken Jerusalem by force. But, inevitably, many would have lost their lives. The Muslims, to avoid unnecessary bloodshed, complied with the conditions. Abū ʿUbayda ﷺ wrote to ʿUmar ﷺ in Madina, who duly set out for Jerusalem leaving behind ʿAlī ﷺ[39] as his deputy.

ʿUmar ﷺ requested all the Muslim generals to meet him at Jābiya, modern-day Nawā near Damascus. The Muslim generals, Yazīd ﷺ, Abū ʿUbayda ﷺ, Khālid ﷺ and ʿAmr ﷺ in the jubilation of meeting their Caliph dressed up and rode out to meet him on fine horses. When ʿUmar ﷺ saw them in their fine, expensive attire he dismounted, picked up pebbles from the ground and started pelting them. He said, 'How quickly have you turned away from your senses! Is it me that you are coming to meet in this attire? You have been eating well for two years. How quickly has gluttony led you astray! By Allah, if you did this at the head of two hundred men, I would have replaced you with others.' The startled generals quickly pointed out that this was only their external attire, and that they still carried weapons with them and had not forgotten their aims and duties. ʿUmar ﷺ, somewhat pacified, joined them and they rode together into Jābiya.

When ʿUmar ﷺ entered Jābiya, a Jew came up to him and said, 'Peace be upon you, O Fārūq! You are the master of Jerusalem. By God, you will not return before God conquers Jerusalem!'[40] While the Companions were sitting together at Jābiya, they became suddenly alarmed and reached for their weapons. ʿUmar ﷺ asked, 'What is it?' There was a cloud of dust being raised on the horizon to which the Companions directed ʿUmar's attention. Horsemen brandishing swords were visible. He said: 'They are seeking assurance of safety. Do not be afraid, but grant it to them.' As the horsemen came closer it became apparent that they were from Jerusalem requesting assurances of safety. ʿUmar ﷺ wrote for them the peace condition:

> *In the name of Allah, the Merciful, the Compassionate.*
>
> This is the assurance of safety, which the servant of Allah, ʿUmar, the Commander of the Faithful, has granted to the people of Aelia (Jerusalem).
>
> He has granted them an assurance of safety for their lives, property, churches, crosses, the sick and the healthy of the city, and for all the rituals that belong to their religion. Their churches will not be inhabited by Muslims and will not be destroyed. Neither they, nor the land on which they stand, nor their crosses, nor their property will be damaged. They will not be forcibly converted. No Jew will live with them in Jerusalem.[41]

> The people of Jerusalem must pay *jizya* like the people of the other cities. As for those who will leave the city, their lives will be safe until they reach their place of safety, and as for those who remain, they will be safe. They will have to pay the *jizya* like the people of Jerusalem. Those of the people of Jerusalem who want to leave with the Byzantines, take their property, and abandon their churches and their crosses will be safe until they reach their place of safety. Those villagers who were in Jerusalem before the killing of so-and-so may remain in the city if they wish, but they must pay *jizya* like the people of Jerusalem. Those who wish may go with the Byzantines, and those who wish may return to their families. Nothing will be taken from them before their harvest is reaped. If they pay the *jizya* according to their obligations, then the contents of this letter are under the covenant of Allah, are the responsibility of His Prophet, of the Caliphs, and the faithful.
>
> The persons who attest to it are: Khālid ibn al-Walid ﵁, ʿAmr ibn al-ʿĀṣ ﵁, ʿAbd al-Raḥmān ibn ʿAwf ﵁ and Muʿāwiya ibn Abī Sufyān ﵁.
>
> This covenant was signed in the year 15 (636-637).[42]

ʿUmar ﵁, the great Caliph, then made his journey to Jerusalem. In striking contrast to Nebuchadnezzar and Titus, he would not desecrate and raze the temple; in contrast to King Saul and Heraclius, he would not usher in religious fanaticism, persecution, and oppression.

In Jābiya, ʿUmar ﵁ prepared to wear his simple, patched attire, mounted on his old horse. The Companions, on seeing his worn clothes and drab horse, thought the Christians in Jerusalem would mock him. They provided a new cloak and a thoroughbred for ʿUmar ﵁. He changed his clothes and mounted the horse but it began to sway. ʿUmar ﷺ dismounted and ordered them to bring back his old horse and simple clothes. In this way, the great Caliph, with his sole servant, made the journey towards Jerusalem. They each took turns to ride the horse while the other walked. When the last furlong approached, it became ʿUmar's turn to walk and his servant to ride. The servant pleaded with ʿUmar ﷺ in every manner but he would not hear of it, and forced his servant to stick to the original agreement. Thus ʿUmar ﷺ, on foot, with great humility and sincerity, entered through the gates of the great city of Jerusalem.

To many Jews, a call to their prayer had been answered. Despite the condition, dictated by the Christians of Jerusalem for the surrender of the city, the Muslims appear to have waived it and for the first time in over six hundred years Jews were allowed to enter Jerusalem. In fact, 70 Jewish families found immediate accommodation within Jerusalem. A document found in the Cairo Genizah reveals that the Jews asked ʿUmar for permission for 200 families to settle in the town. As the patriarch strongly opposed the action, ʿUmar fixed the number of Jewish families at 70.[43]

The many Christians and pagans were also at ease as they were allowed total freedom in following any sect they wished without fear of persecution. Thus Jerusalem was transformed into a pluralist city for the first time in its history.

With the modern Zionist attempts to Judaize Jerusalem, it is important to realize that the Muslims did not liberate Jerusalem from the Jews but from the Christians. Similarly it was the Jews and other minority sects who were the major beneficiaries of the Muslim liberation of the city.

At the time the Bishop, Sophronius, came to the gates to welcome ʿUmar ﷺ. When he saw ʿUmar ﷺ, he said, 'In truth this is the abomination of the desolation established in the holy place, which Daniel ﷺ the Prophet spoke of.'[44] The first request ʿUmar ﷺ made was to be taken to the precinct of al-Aqṣā Mosque.

This is not surprising as the significance of al-Aqṣā for Muslims begins from the Prophet Adam ﷺ and continues through the Prophet Dāwūd (David) ﷺ. The Prophet Dāwūd ﷺ united the scattered tribes of Israel and captured Jerusalem. The Prophet Sulaymān (Soloman) ﷺ inherited the kingdom from his father, the Prophet Dāwūd ﷺ, and built a place of worship on the hills of Moriah. After the Prophet Sulaymān's death the kingdom split into two parts, Israel in the north and Judah including Jerusalem in the south. After 200 years of rivalry, Israel was conquered by a ruler from al-Sham. The temple was gradually despoiled and the pure teachings of the Prophet Mūsā (Moses) ﷺ corrupted. Nebuchadnezzar in 586 BC captured Jerusalem and razed the temple to the ground. In 536 BC, the Persians captured Jerusalem and allowed the reconstruction of the second temple. Around 300 BC the Greeks captured Jerusalem. They dedicated the temple to Zeus and began sacrificing pigs on its altar. In 164 BC the Hasmonean Jews captured the temple and ruled it for a century. In 63 BC Herod was appointed King of Judea. He slaughtered the Hasmoneans and claimed guardianship of the temple. A period of oppression and barbarism followed and in this period the Prophet ʿĪsā (Jesus) ﷺ was born. His mission was to bring the people back to the teachings of the Prophets Ibrāhīm ﷺ and Mūsā ﷺ.

After ʿĪsā ﷺ, years of riots and massacres followed over the control of the temple. In 70 AD, the Roman Emperor Titus captured Jerusalem and reduced the temple to rubble. A new city named Aelia was built on the ruins of Jerusalem with a temple dedicated to Jupiter. In 324 the Roman Emperor Constantine became a Christian and many Churches were built in Jerusalem. For a short period in 620 the Persians captured Jerusalem and massacred the Christians. The temple site remained in ruins for hundreds of years and was used as a rubbish tip. The Jews who were banished from Jerusalem for nearly 600 years (apart from the few years of Persian rule) were given renewed access under the Islamic rule.

Muslims consider al-Aqṣā to have been first built by Ādam ؑ. Reference is drawn from the *ḥadīth* recorded in Muslim that Abū Dharr stated: I asked the Messenger of Allah ﷺ about the first mosque on earth. 'The Sacred Mosque (in Makka),' he replied. 'Which next?' I asked. 'Al-Aqṣā Mosque,' he said. 'And how long was it between them?' I asked. 'Forty years,' the Prophet ﷺ replied.

When the gates to the holy sanctuary were opened ʿUmar ؓ turned towards the *miḥrāb* of the Prophet Dāwūd ؑ (David)[45] and prostrated the prostration of Dāwūd,[46] and thereafter performed two *rakʿa ṣalāh* (units of prayer). In the first *rakʿah* he recited *Sūra Ṣād,* 38[47] and in the next *rakʿa Sūra Banī Isrā'īl,* 17.[48]

Thereafter he called for Kaʿb ؓ and asked, 'Where do you think we should establish the place of prayer (mosque)?' Kaʿb ؓ said, 'Place the mosque behind the Rock.' ʿUmar ؓ disagreed as this would mean people having to stand behind the rock in order to face the *qibla*[49] and thus people might start to venerate the rock.[50] Thus ʿUmar ؓ built the Mosque with its *qibla* in front of the rock. ʿUmar ؓ then stood up and went to the rubbish which the Byzantines had left in the compound of al-Aqṣā.

He said, 'O People!, do what I am doing.' He knelt down in the midst of the rubbish and gathered it by the handful into the lower part of his mantle.[51] The Companions followed suit and worked throughout the day until all the rubbish accumulated by the Byzantines was cleared. ʿUmar ؓ then ordered the construction of a mosque whereon stands today's elegant black-domed al-Aqṣā Mosque.

The *adhān* (call to prayer) is said to have been called during ʿUmar's ؓ stay in Jerusalem; Bilāl ibn Rabāḥ the first *mu'adhdhin* in Islam (also called the Prophet's *mu'adhdhin*) was, at some point, requested by ʿUmar ﵁ to give the *adhān*. He complied even though he had promised never to call the *adhān* after the Prophet's ﷺ demise. When the Companions heard his inspiring voice, vivid memories of the Golden Era in Madina with the beloved Prophet ﷺ came flooding back to them and many were reduced to tears. Whether Bilāl ﵁ gave the first *adhān* in Masjid al-Aqṣā is not certain, but he definitely called the *adhān* in al-Aqṣā during ʿUmar's stay in Jerusalem.

It appears Sophronius took to ʿUmar ﵁ and offered him a robe and a loincloth as gifts. ʿUmar ﵁ initially refused but on the persistence of the Bishop, compromised and agreed to wear the new clothes while his old ones were being washed. When ʿUmar ﵁ received his clothes back, he returned the robe and loincloth to the Bishop. On one occasion when the Bishop was giving ʿUmar ﵁ a tour of Jerusalem, the time for prayer – *ṣalāh* – approached when they were in the Church of the Sepulchre. The Bishop suggested that ʿUmar ﵁ perform the prayer in the church but ʿUmar ﵁ with foresight and humility declined. He feared that if he performed his *ṣalāh* in the church, future generations of Muslims might on the pretext of following in his footsteps, also enter the Church to perform *ṣalāh* and that this could lead to inconveniences, harassment and possible confiscation of the Church.

ʿUmar ﵁ spent a few weeks – reports vary from 10 to 40 days – in Jerusalem, attending to state, civil and personal matters before returning to Madina with the same simplicity he had entered Jerusalem.

While ʿUmar ﵁ was in Jerusalem, Tamīm al-Dārī ﵁, a Companion of the Prophet who had travelled from Hebron to Madina in 9 and accepted Islam, presented a document to ʿUmar from the Prophet. The document promised Tamīm al-Dārī ﵁ *waqf* (religious endowment) of land around Hebron, upon the liberation of Palestine by the Muslims. ʿUmar ﵁

granted Tamīm ﷺ the promised area around Hebron but after dividing it into three parts: one third for Tamīm and his family, a second third for the poor and the wayfarers, and the last third to be built on by the people.[52] Mahmūd Ibrāhīm in *Faḍā'il al-Quds* (Virtues of Jerusalem), states that Tamīm ﷺ became the governor of Jerusalem after the reign of the Caliph ʿUthmān.

The Muslims easily liberated the remaining area of Palestine after the conquest of Jerusalem. It is not clear which commander was responsible for which towns. However, it is generally maintained that Shuraḥbīl ibn Ḥasana ﷺ moved to the south into what is now Jordan and ʿAmr ibn al-ʿĀṣ ﷺ towards the towns of Gaza and Ramla.

Caesarea (Qayṣarīya) on the Mediterranean coast was subdued after a prolonged siege of around seven years. It is possible several commanders were involved and this has rather confused the historical records. However, Balādhurī maintains that the original siege was masterminded by ʿAmr ﷺ. ʿAmr ﷺ would camp outside the city walls and whenever his assistance was requested by the other Muslim generals he would go to their aid. In this manner he assisted in the battles from Ajnadayn to Yarmuk, and in the liberation of Jerusalem, while the siege was being maintained around Caesarea. After he left for Egypt, the siege was continued by Abū ʿUbayda ﷺ until his death in the plague of Amwās. Yazīd ibn Abī Sufyān ﷺ was appointed governor of al-Sham and after his death he was succeeded by his brother, Muʿāwiya ﷺ.

Palestine was divided into two provinces and ʿUmar ﷺ appointed ʿAlqama ibn Ḥakīm ﷺ and ʿAlqama ibn Mujazziz ﷺ in charge of them. The governors were stationed at Ramla and Jerusalem respectively.

Although the chronology of battles is difficult to ascertain, this should not be used as a pretext for discrediting Islamic historians. The advance in al-Sham was complicated by several factors. Firstly, there were four generals operating in al-Sham at any one time and more than one battle at any given instance could have been taking place. Secondly, the major cities, like Damascus, were fortified and though Muslim forces were besieging them simply by encamping outside the walls, other battles were being waged in other areas at the same time. Thirdly, Muslim forces, which had to evacuate some cities after initial occupation (Damascus, Ḥimṣ) because of Byzantine counter-attacks, reoccupied them, for a second time, after the Battle of Yarmuk. Further, dates on some surrender documents, as in the case of Damascus were recorded after an interval, which led to discrepancies. These are most probably some of the reasons why one city is recorded as being occupied on two different dates. The richness of Islamic sources must be appreciated in the face of the few paragraphs left by the Byzantines to cover the collapse of over half of the Byzantium Empire.

As the Romans regarded only themselves as civilized and everyone east of the Mediterranean Sea as barbarians, it would be demeaning to profess and record a defeat at their hands. The Muslim scholars' emphasis has been on the method and nature of events rather than the chronology. As such, different original authors (al-Azdī, Balādhurī, Ibn Isḥāq, al-Wāqidī and al-Ṭabarī) may not have been able to record the sequence of events accurately, but they have left us a wealth of information regarding the conduct of the Muslims. Moreover their scholarship is sufficient to enable us to reconstruct the Muslims' liberation of al-Sham.

NOTES

1. Kaegi, Walter, *Byzantium and the Early Islamic Conquests* (Cambridge, 1992), p. 67.
2. Balādhurī states that Abū Bakr ﷺ wanted to give overall command to Abū ʿUbayda ﷺ, but the latter begged to be relieved. The claim by others that he did confer overall command on Abū ʿUbayda ﷺ is not confirmed.

3. Al-Wāqidī states ʿAmr 🕮 was given oral instructions to lead the prayers in case the armies unite and to have each commander lead the prayers of his own army when the armies are separate.

4. The higher figures estimated in some sources are unlikely both on account of the scarcity of manpower and the need to travel at speed across the desert.

5. This advice is from the Messenger of Allah 🕮 quoted in a *ḥadīth* of al-Bukhārī.

6. According to al-Ṭabarī, after each day's travel they pressed water out of ten camels for every group of horses.

7. On the authority of Ibn Isḥāq in al-Ṭabarī, 'Ta'rikh al-Ṭabarī', *The History of al-Ṭabarī*, Vol. XI, 'The Challenge to the Empires'. Trans. Khālid Yahya Blankinship. (Albany, State Uni. of New York, 1993), p. 122.

8. This part of the history related by al-Ṭabarī (d. 310 AH) is taken almost verbatim from Sayf's work (d. approx. 170 AH). Sayf's full name is Abū ʿAbdullāh Sayf b. ʿUmar al-Usaydī al-Tamīmī. Although a Sunnī, his authority has been questioned on three counts: 1. Most of his authorities in *isnād* are unknown (*majhūlūn*) to other commentators. 2. He sometimes extended a chain of transmitters back an additional generation by adding the nameless father of the earliest transmitter to the beginning of the chain. 3. He has a tendency to exaggerate the roles of certain Companions in the early conquests, and to embellish his work with the exploits of other, imaginary Companions and with heroes whom he invented, especially to represent his own tribal group. For more details see al-Ṭabarī, op. cit., Vol. XI, p. xxiii. As is pointed out by Khālid Yahya Blankinship, our assessment of Sayf in no way undermines the work of classical *ʿUlamā'* of the past and present as they realised Sayf's work was suspicious and have quoted so unequivocally. 'In fact the condemnation of Sayf by the *ʿUlamā'* ought to serve as a reminder to modern scholars that ancient political or religious climate did not bias the true Muslims and that the search for the truth had its place in earlier times as well as in our own.' The great Muslim scholar al-Dhahabī, in his book *Mīzān al-Iʿtidāl* quotes the views of authentic Muslim scholars on Sayf. Shaykh Yahya ibn Saʿīd [the Imām of Shaykh Bukhārī] states that Sayf is a weak narrator. Imām Abū Dāwūd placed 'no value on Sayf's authority'. Shaykh al-Dhahabī himself says his *isnād* is incomplete. I have quoted Sayf as many academics have used Sayf's work to prove their point and it will be of interest for investigative individuals to know the original source of some of the modern-day debates. Wherever I have quoted Sayf I have also attempted to cite other historians.

9. The place called 'Quraqir' has not been identified, although Donner considers it to be Qulban Qirajir, 500 km. southwest of ʿAyn al-Tamr.

10. This date has been given on the authority of Abū Jaʿfar, also quoted by al-Ṭabarī, op. cit., Vol. XI, p. 109.

11. Donner, Fred McGraw, *The Early Islamic Conquests* (Princeton, 1981), p. 129.

12. Balādhurī, al-Imām Abū-l ʿAbbas Aḥmad ibn Jābir, *Kitāb Futūḥ Al-Buldān, The Origins of the Islamic State.* Trans. Phillip Khuri Hitti. (Beirut, Khayats, 1966), p. 174.
13. Balādhurī states that this battle took place in the last days of Jumādā al-Ūlā, others place it a few days later in early Jumādā al-Thānī. Al-Ṭabarī records it as Saturday, 28th Jumāda al-Ūlā (30 July 634). Western writers in order to show a greater disagreement among Muslim historians tend to also quote Sayf (see footnote 89) who places the Battle of Ajnadayn after Yarmuk and just before the surrender of Jerusalem.
14. Fihl is ancient Pella, east of the river Jordan. It is now the site of extensive ruins and a popular tourist attraction.
15. This refers to individuals who preferred to fight rather than pay the *jizya*.
16. Ibn Isḥāq and Balādhurī, have both quoted this.
17. Al-Wāqidī's full name is Abū ʿAbdullāh Muḥammad ibn ʿUmar al-Wāqidī [b. 130 AH]. He expended great efforts to collecting material on the life of the Prophet ﷺ and the battles of the early Muslims. He writes that he did not omit to contact a single son of the *Ṣaḥāba*, or those martyred on the battlefields. Al-Wāqidī not only recorded from these individuals but asked them to take him to where these events took place. Ibn Nadīm states, al-Wāqidī employed two people to work daily taking notes. His library can be gauged by the fact that he left 600 boxes of books, each box requiring two men to carry it. He wrote more than 28 books, the most famous on warfare.
18. According to other reports: one night the Byzantines carried a corpse out through the Jābiya Gate, while some of their soldiers guarded the entrance waiting for the return of their comrades. However, Abū ʿUbayda ﷺ seeing an opportunity attacked the soldiers at the gate. After a prolonged battle he overpowered them and entered the city.
19. *Ghanīma* (booty) is what Muslims seize in fighting. *Ghanīma* is divided so that one-fifth is given to the head of state (caliph) to be distributed as mentioned in the Qur'ān (8: 41) – the near of kin, orphans, and wayfarer – and the remaining four-fifths belongs to the Muslims who captured it, to be distributed equally with no distinction between rank. Whereas *jizya* and *kharāj* are taxes that the exchequer of the Muslim state receives under the terms and conditions of the peace treaty. Further, the inhabitants of a territory taken by force can lose claim to their assets. Hence, territory taken peacefully enjoys far more rights than that taken by force and the Muslim soldiers do not gain any material wealth thereby.
20. *Mishkāt al-Maṣābīḥ* on the authority of Mālik.
21. Quoted by Balādhurī.
22. Al-Ṭabarī quotes on the authority of Abū al-Zahrā' al-Qushayrī.

23. Al-Ṭabarī on the authority of Sayf recounts the events differently: Heraclius, observing the Muslims from Antioch, decided to send four different battalions to check the four respective Muslim Commanders. The Muslims on learning of the huge military force took counsel from Madina. Abū Bakr ﷺ ordered them to unite under one banner at Yarmuk. A letter to this effect attributed to Abū Bakr ﷺ is also often quoted.
24. Balādhurī, op. cit., p. 211.
25. Stratos, Andreas N., *Byzantium in the Seventh Century*, Vol. I, pp. 602-634. Trans. Marc Ogilvie Grant (Amsterdam, 1968), p. 66.
26. Al-Ṭabarī on the authority of Sayf states that Theodore, the brother of Heraclius was appointed to the supreme command. However this is contrary to Ibn Isḥāq. According to Theophanes (*The Chronicles of Theophanes*. Trans. Harry Turtledove (Philadelphia, 1982), p. 37) it was a different person of the same name who was the Sakellarois (Keeper of the Purse) and not Heraclius' brother, Theodore.
27. Kaegi, Walter, op. cit., p. 119.
28. Ibid., p. 136.
29. Ibid., p. 124.
30. Al-Ṭabarī on the authority of Sayf states Khālid ibn al-Walīd ﷺ was the overall commander.
31. Balādhurī, op. cit., Among the ladies was Hind, wife of Abū Sufyān, mother of Muʿāwiya, the daughter of ʿUtba, who admonished the soldiers of Islam to fight to the last.
32. For the full list of the deceased see Balādhurī, op. cit., p. 208. Al-Ṭabarī on the authority of Sayf, states three thousand Muslims died in the battle (Vol. XI, p. 100). Al-Ṭabarī on the authority of Ibn Isḥāq (Vol. XII, p. 134).
33. Abū Sufyān was the leading chief of the Quraysh and fought against the Prophet ﷺ in the battles before the Conquest of Makka. At the time of Makka's liberation it was his house (and the Holy Mosque) that were appointed by the Prophet ﷺ to be a safe haven. On his conversion he became totally committed to the cause of Islam and ventured out to Yarmuk when he was over 70 years of age, while his son Yazīd was one of the four leading Commanders.
34. Al-Ṭabarī who on Sayf's authority, considers the battle of Yarmuk to have been the first encounter with the Byzantines, states that the battle was won ten days after the death of Abū Bakr ﷺ, i.e. 5 Jumāda al-Thānī 13/6, August 634.
35. Al-Ṭabarī, 'Ta'rikh al-Ṭabarī', *The History of al-Ṭabarī*, Vol. XII, 'The Battle of al-Qādisiya and the Conquest of al-Sham and Palestine'. Trans. Yohanan Friedmann. (Albany, State Uni. of New York, 1992), p. 182.
36. Balādhurī reports it was Abū ʿUbayda ﷺ himself who sacked Qinnaṣrīn.
37. Balādhurī, op. cit., p. 226.

38. There is another report which states the occupants of Antioch rebelled while Abū ʿUbayda ﵁ was in Palestine. When he heard the news he despatched ʿAmr ibn al-ʿĀṣ ﵁ who quelled the rebellion and returned to Jerusalem. Upon analysis, this report cannot be taken seriously.
39. According to al-Ṭabarī, ʿAlī ﵁ was appointed deputy and al-Yaʿqūbī mentions ʿUthmān ﵁.
40. The reason the Bishop of Jerusalem requested to be allowed to surrender to al-Fārūq (ʿUmar) was to fulfil the prophecy of the Scriptures, which predicted: 'Rejoice O Jerusalem! al-Fārūq will come to you and cleanse you.' (See al-Ṭabarī, Vol. XII, p. 196.)
41. The sentence 'No Jew will live with them in Jerusalem' was a condition set by the Christians in order to maintain the *status quo*. The Christians were concerned that the Jews who had been banished might be allowed to return by the Muslims. ʿUmar ﵁, however, did allow them entry into Jerusalem as and when they wanted to, thus bringing to an end 600 years of exile (Theophanes, *Chronicles*, op. cit., p. 39) and Michael the Syrian state that the Bishop of Jerusalem, Sophronius made a treaty with ʿUmar ﵁ forbidding Jews to live in Jerusalem. See Donner, op. cit., note 287, p. 322. Also see Andrew Palmer, *The Seventh Century in West Syrian Chronicles*, Trans. Andrew Palmer (Liverpool, Liverpool University Press, 1993), p. 113: ... 'as (the Bishop) desired concerning their churches and their customs. They accepted the amnesty and the oaths concerning Palestine. The stipulation was made that no Jew might live in Jerusalem'.
42. Al-Ṭabarī, Vol. XII, p. 192. Balādhurī states 17. However, Bishop Sophronius who surrendered the city died in March 638. See Stratos, op. cit., note XII.
43. *Encyclopaedia Judaica* (Jerusalem, 1972), p. 1409.
44. Theophanes, op. cit., p. 39.
45. Dāwūd's ﵇ *miḥrāb* is mentioned in the Qur'ān, *Sūra Ṣād* 38: 21, 'And has the news of the litigants reached you? When they climbed over the wall into (his) *miḥrāb* (a prayer place)...'

    As one faces the *qibla* the *Miḥrāb* was probably located to the far left of al-Aqṣā Mosque in al-Marwān quarter or just beyond, where the earthquake of the Fatimid period claimed the land.
46. Qur'ān 38: 24, '...Then he (Dāwūd) sought forgiveness of his Lord and fell down bowing, and he repented.' For the full *tafsir* (commentary) see *The Qur'ān Tafsīr-E-ʿUthmānī*.
47. *Sūra Ṣād* narrates the story of the Prophet Dāwūd (David) ﵇ and the Prophet Sulaymān (Soloman) ﵇.
48. *Sūra Banī Isrā'īl* makes clear the centrality for Islam of Bayt al-Maqdis (the Furthest Mosque) and Jerusalem. It was from the Furthest Mosque in Jerusalem that the literal ascension of the Prophet ﷺ took place, through the seven heavens up to the Sublime Throne. It reads: 'Glory to Allah, Who

did take His servant for a journey by night from the Sacred Mosque to the Furthest Mosque (al-Aqṣā), whose precincts We did Bless – in order that We might show him some of Our signs: for He is the One Who hears and sees (all things)...'

49. The direction Muslims face when they perform *ṣalāh*. Up until 2, Muslims faced Bayt al-Maqdis and thereafter a revelation in the Qur'ān was made for a change of direction in favour of the Ka'ba in Makka.
50. In the centre of the Noble Sanctuary lies a huge rock on which the Prophet ﷺ is assumed to have stood before making the ascension to the heavens. This entire Sanctuary was also the first *qibla* of the Muslims. At the end of the seventh century, the Umayyad Caliph, 'Abdul Mālik ibn Marwān, ordered the construction of the Mosque over the rock. The construction became one of the most beautiful features of Jerusalem. Today the skyline of Jerusalem glitters with the golden Dome of the Rock, its most distinctive and famous landmark.
51. Al-Ṭabarī, Vol. XII, p. 197.
52. Abdallah el-Khatib, *British Journal of Middle Eastern Studies*, Vol. 28, No. 1, May 2001, p. 30.

4

Deciphering Victory

An objective accounting of the Byzantine defeat at the hands of Muslims who have been caricatured as savages and troglodytes has posed great difficulties for some historians. The early orientalists branded Muslims as wild mobs, brandishing the sword in one hand and the Qur'ān in the other, destroying all who came in their way. Over time, these caricatures, in deep denial of Muslim merits and achievements, sowed the seeds of what is now called Islamophobia. Yet others proposed different theories: Muslims need to divert manpower outward in order to prevent internal conflict; scarcity of food and arable lands in the Peninsula – which, not too subtly, depict the Muslims as motivated by worldly gains. Still other theories, again denying any virtue to the Muslims, point to the weaknesses in the Byzantine forces and their shortcomings. It is no doubt arguable that the empire was overstretched, lost its governance and exhausted the will to continue, a process that has seen many empires before and since decline and fade.

However, there are two major questions that need to be investigated. The first, what motivated the Muslims to advance into al-Sham? The second, equally important, what are the reasons for their success?

MOTIVES

It must be borne in mind that Islam is a missionary religion, and the Prophet Muḥammad ﷺ inculcated this aspect of Islam into his followers from the beginning. The concept and philosophy of *dār al-Islām* (literally, the 'abode of peace' territory under Islamic rule) and *dār al-ḥarb* (non-Islamic territory or literally the 'abode of war') was established very early on. Only later, during the ʿAbbāsid Caliphate, as the study of *Siyar* (international law) developed did the concept of *dār al-ʿahd* (land of treaty), *dār al-ṣulḥ* (land of safety) and *dār al-ḥiyād* (land of neutrality) come to the fore. The vision of establishing an Islamic al-Sham was implanted very early on by the Prophet Muḥammad ﷺ. Central to that vision was the sanctity of Jerusalem and the need to unite the two houses of the Lord, the Kaʿba in Makka and al-Aqṣā in Jerusalem, under Islamic rule.

Jerusalem just like Makka is a holy place. Its merits derive from three sources: the Qurʾān where there are 70 direct and indirect references, the many *aḥādīth* (sayings of the noble Prophet ﷺ) that glorify Jerusalem and the *waqf* (religious endowment) made to Tamīm al-Dārī ﵁.

The sanctity of Jerusalem was affirmed during the Makkan period in the night journey of the Prophet Muḥammad ﷺ called the *Miʿrāj*. The *Miʿrāj* is agreed by most scholars to have taken place on the 27th night of the month of Rajab, one year before the *Hijra*. This physical journey by the Prophet from Makka to Jerusalem and thereafter to the upper heavens, links the two holy sites within the embrace of Islam.

There are numerous *aḥādīth* in all the Six Books (the most widely accepted 'canonical' compilations which form the Prophet's sayings), which extol the importance of Jerusalem in particular and al-Sham in general.

In 9/631 a religious Christian, Tamīm al-Dārī from al-Khalīl (modern-day Hebron) in Palestine, travelled to Madina and accepted Islam at the hands of the Prophet ﷺ. He lived in Madina until the death of the third Caliph, ʿUthmān ؓ and then moved to Jerusalem. The Prophet ﷺ bestowed upon him four localities in the area of Hebron. Tamīm al-Dārī ؓ spent his final years there until he died in 40/660.

He asked the Prophet ﷺ to grant him these areas near Jerusalem when they came under Muslim rule. The Prophet ﷺ agreed to grant him those areas as a *waqf* on condition that they could not be sold to anybody. Tamīm ؓ asked the Prophet ﷺ to write for him a document confirming the grant. When Jerusalem was captured during the era of the second Caliph, ʿUmar ؓ, Tamīm ؓ submitted the Prophet's document and ʿUmar honoured the promise.[1]

Further, in the year 5 during the Battle of al-Khandaq (the Trench), the Prophet ﷺ came to the assistance of Salmān al-Fārisī ؓ, who had come across a rock while digging the trench. When the Prophet Muḥammad ﷺ struck the rock with a pickaxe a flashing light emanated from the rock. This happened three times in succession. The Prophet ﷺ explained to Salmān, 'The first means that Allah has opened up to me Yemen, the second al-Sham and third the East.'

The liberation of Jerusalem and al-Sham was implanted within the Muslim mind, but the fulfilment of that aspiration needed a stimulus. As the teaching of Islam indicate there is a reason behind every outcome.

The first direct confrontation with the Byzantine Empire began as early as in the year 8 when the Prophet ﷺ despatched a battalion for the Battle of Mu'ta. Thereafter, the expedition of Tabuk must have further alerted the Byzantines to contemplating action against the growing influence of Madina. After Heraclius' victory over the Persians, his continued presence in al-Sham, and his making Antioch the headquarters, the Muslims were rightly apprehensive. This is reflected in an authentic *ḥadīth* relating to ʿUmar ؓ quoted both in Bukhārī and *Ṣaḥīḥ* Muslim, which states: '... A Companion of mine suddenly began knocking the door, shouting, "Open! Open!" I asked: "Have the Romans[2] come?"'

The Prophet's ﷺ decision, days before his death, to despatch young Usāma ؓ on a reconnaissance mission along the borders further substantiated the Muslims' disquiet about the Byzantines and the need to learn of their intentions.

Upon the Prophet's ﷺ death, the nascent *Umma* was put under great strain by apostates, hypocrites and false prophets. Numerous battalions were despatched to deal with these. Khālid ibn al-Walīd ؓ was sent against Ṭulayḥa, ʿIkrima ؓ against Musajlama, Muhājir ؓ against Mahra and ʿAmr ؓ against Banī Khuzāʿa. The effect was an exhaustion of manpower in Madina. Whilst the Muslim army was checking apostates, many new converts, clinging to their old habits, refused to pay *zakāh* and, once more, Abū Bakr ؓ had to despatch what remained of the army against them, until they complied.

In Muḥarram 12/18 March-16 April 633, Khālid ibn al-Walīd ؓ was ordered to march towards Persia. Later the same year, Abū Bakr ؓ was forced, under the assumed threat of a Byzantine attack, to send another Khālid ؓ, Khālid ibn Saʿīd ؓ, to survey the Byzantine frontier, even while the Muslims were actively engaged in conflict with the Persian forces in the east.

After Khālid ibn Saʿīd's debacle, Madina appeared to the Muslims to be exposed and in imminent danger of an attack. The threat to Madina was real and, more importantly, the Companions believed it. Thus to advance to al-Sham in order to check any infiltration by the Byzantine forces disturbed by Khālid ؓ, whether by accident or not, forms a most significant motive.

Further, the first generation Muslims considered it their duty to educate and inculcate in the people of the world the divine way of life prescribed by the Creator. However, the *daʿwa* (missionary work) was to take a prescribed path, which was to be peaceful and non-coercive. The Prophet Muḥammad ﷺ himself began inviting the neighbouring leaders, including Heraclius, by means of letters and envoys. After him, the Companions carried forward his deeds in person. To the Muslims the duty to inform the world of Islam, to enjoin good and forbid evil, irrespective of creed, culture or colour is a key responsibility. For devout Muslims of the first generation, and for the pious Muslim ever since, to save a fellow human from the dangers of hell has been the prime reason and object of life. The Companions' compassion and concern to serve mankind cannot be underestimated. It was arguably a further reason for moving to neighbouring al-Sham. It must be stated that the duty of performing *daʿwa* was answered by the Companions through profession of the message to those they met and through the righteousness of their conduct. This is substantiated in a detailed study by Courbage and Fargues in which they cite that, by the end of the first century after conquest, only 6 per cent of the population in al-Sham were Muslims. This represents approximately 250,000 out of a total population of 4 million people.[3] If force had been used or the sole motive of conquerors had been to proselytise, then the initial census would have definitely shown a higher percentage of Muslims.

There are two major accusations levelled against the Muslims for moving into al-Sham, which need careful examination.

Firstly, that the Muslims advanced into al-Sham to enrich themselves. Several arguments can be presented against this. If there was a need to migrate from the Ḥijāz into al-Sham for financial gain then, unfortunately for the advocates of this theory, there is absolutely no evidence whatever of a mass migration of Arabs into al-Sham during or immediately after the conquests. Further, the evidence from both Graeco-Syriac and Arabic sources reports of no looting or pillaging by the Muslim forces, to substantiate the 'lust for booty' theory.

In fact, the Muslim forces sacrificed the opportunity for material wealth in Damascus and other towns of al-Sham. Their fair and just government ensured a plea for their return when they had to evacuate the towns of Damascus, Ḥimṣ and Ba'labak. The fact that only 6 per cent of the total population of al-Sham had become Muslim after one hundred years needs to be reiterated. The proponents of the economic theory point towards the Muslims moving towards the prosperous al-Sham rather than poor Africa in the south. This is mainly because the south posed no threat to Islam, as the king of Abyssinia had accepted the message of Islam. Furthermore, the Muslims were not keen to traverse the waterways at this early stage, as may be noted by 'Umar's ﷺ refusal of Mu'āwiya's proposal of a sea-faring expedition to Cyprus.

The history books are full of anecdotes referring to the Companions' contempt for wealth and none more so than the leaders themselves. The Caliph Abū Bakr ﷺ distributed all the spoils of war as soon as they arrived in Madina, to the poor. Once someone suggested to him that the *Bayt al-Māl* (Public Treasury) be kept locked and under guard. He said, 'The Treasury incurs no dangers as it remains almost empty for nothing is left undistributed.' Upon his death, the Companions went to check the *Bayt al-Māl* only to find it devoid of anything of value. However after a search, a single coin was discovered under a chest. The first Caliph was the embodiment of austerity. Not even the most ardent of his critics can point to a single fault in this regard. Shortly before his death he called upon the Companions to calculate what addition to his wealth was made after he became the Caliph. They found one assistant who looked after the children, a she-camel and one sheet of cloth. The family were ordered to send the three possessions to 'Umar ﷺ when he took office. Abū Bakr further returned to the public treasury every dirham, drawn[4] by him as Caliph, which was then promptly distributed to the poor. ʿUmar ﷺ followed in the footsteps of his predecessor. He was found on many occasions to be weeping when the booty from Persia and Byzantine arrived in Madina. When questioned about it he used to say: 'I have heard the Prophet ﷺ say, "When worldly conquest is conferred upon a community, Allah the Exalted puts into their hearts enmity and malice until the Day of Judgement," and I am afraid of this.' He further used to pray: 'O Allah! I seek refuge in You from this (abundance of wealth) lest it be a point of testing ʿUmar.' He counselled the Companions by reciting from the Qur'ān:

> *Do they think that because We have granted them abundance of wealth and sons, We would hasten them on in every good? Nay they do not perceive* (al-Mu'minūn 23: 55-6).

The examples are simply too many to recall and would require another volume to set down in writing. A final anecdote of the Muslims' indifference to worldly gains and their perpetual consciousness of the Hereafter is transmitted by the eminent Islamic scholar, Imām Aḥmad. He reports that when ʿUmar ﷺ arrived in al-Sham, he asked to be taken to Abū ʿUbayda's house. ʿUmar ﷺ found nothing but a sword, a shield and a camel's saddle. ʿUmar ﷺ asked him: 'Have you not taken what your other companions have?' Abū ʿUbayda replied: 'O Amīr al-Mu'minīn! It is (the contents) enough for me to reach my bedroom (grave)!'[5]

The second accusation levelled against the Muslims is that there was a surplus of population, which required to be relocated and get them preoccupied with the service of Islam. The evidence cited so far indicates both Abū Bakr ﷺ and ʿUmar ﷺ had a recruitment problem necessitating requests to tribal leaders from all over Arabia. The shortage was so acute that it required the transfer of forces from the Persian to the Byzantine front and vice versa as the need arose. In the decisive Battle of Yarmuk where the Muslims faced the united might of the Byzantine Empire, only around 30,000 were assembled. The offer of financial inducements to those non-Muslims who supported the Muslims is well recorded. But yet again, there are no demographic records showing a migration of Arabs from Arabia into al-Sham to justify this assertion. In fact both Abū Bakr ﷺ and ʿUmar ﷺ issued well-documented edicts, refusing the Companions of the Prophet ﷺ, permission to leave Madina.

SUCCESS

The most perplexing task is to explain coherently how a band of unknown illiterates, hitherto engrossed in tribal fights managed so quickly to establish themselves as a cohesive, disciplined force, capable of confronting and defeating the strongest military powers of their time.

The Roman and Persian Empires had been rivals, and often at war, for generations. The province area of al-Sham was in disarray in the early part of the seventh century. By 9/630 Heraclius had restored Byzantine authority once again over al-Sham, so that it was safe for him to visit Jerusalem. Between 9 and 13 when the first confrontation took place with the Muslim army, Heraclius had 4 years in which to reinforce and re-organize his forces and the empire. To assume that the mighty Byzantine army lay prostrate is a gross distortion of the historical facts. This is borne out by the fact that when the Muslims arrived in Mu'ta as early as 8, they were confronted with a large and well-trained army.

The factors against the Byzantine Empire at the time must include friction in the church, disquiet amongst the citizens about Heraclius' marriage to his niece, which was perceived as incest, the heavy taxation, and the reduction or, in some cases, late payment of civil salaries. These factors can be summed up as a decline in social order, justice, economic potential and general weakening of the ability to govern.

However, it was in these very same socio-economic conditions, which had led to the Byzantine expulsion of the Persians from their empire, that made the Muslim success all the more astounding.

The most important factors emanating from an objective analysis indicate that the success of the Muslims lay in transforming the political and socio-economic regime so as to allow personal freedom in all spheres, without state interference or religious persecution, coupled with economic incentives by way of fair taxation and enterprise. Under the rule of Islam, the people enjoyed a degree of religious freedom, and economic relief, justice and recourse to law, as well as the lifting of unfair taxes, that they had not experienced before. That is why the Islamic conquest and Islamic rule endured.

It is Islam alone, through its revolutionary teachings that imbued the Arabs with moral character, cohesion and devotion that brought about the remarkable and enduring changes in the history of former Byzantine provinces and, eventually in world history.

The factors instrumental in the success of the Muslims include:

1. Religious Cohesion

Until the advent of Islam, Arabian society was fragmented and divided. Tribalism and feudal disputes influenced much of daily life. It was through the inherent universal ideals of Islam that tribalism was weakened and replaced by a new order based on piety (service to Islam) rather than on nepotism or cronyism.

The united force of Arabia under Islam with the object of propagating the word of the Lord and safeguarding their beliefs propelled the Muslims into the neighbouring territories. Islam swept aside the internal animosities inherited from their forefathers and for the first time the tribes of Quraysh, al-Anṣār, Thaqīf and even the earlier tribes who had apostatised or rebelled immediately after the Prophet's ﷺ death, like al-Ashʿath ibn Qays were united. Islam, through the Qur'ān and the practical example of the Prophet Muḥammad ﷺ, provided a pattern upon which Abū Bakr ؓ, ʿUmar ؓ and the other Companions modelled their conduct. The teachings of *tawḥīd*, *risāla,* and *ākhira* – i.e., to affirm belief in and worship of only one God, to believe in all His prophets culminating in the final prophethood of Muḥammad ﷺ and to believe in a life after this worldly life where we will be judged and then punished or rewarded accordingly – coupled with a personal duty to ensure the safety and advancement of Islam, formed the cornerstone of the unification of Muslim society.

The most intractable groups within Arabian society were the nomads. The early Caliphs, through the teachings of the Prophet ﷺ, integrated them through inter-marriage, and by appointing them to administrative posts and joint expeditions. This won over their hearts and even the nomads were brought into the mainstream society.

In the Byzantine Empire, diametrically opposite socio-religious factors were at work. There existed a sharp divide in the religious beliefs between the ruling elite and the general population of al-Sham and in particular the Ghassānid confederates who were Monophysites. This division was exacerbated during the reigns of Maurice and Phocas. Heraclius, for a time, did manage to reach a compromise on some of the religious difficulties by honouring and considering as brothers in religion his confederates who were Monophysites. But the great differences that existed prior to Heraclius between the Graeco-Roman rulers and their confederates were slowly re-emerging. Old feuds were simmering just beneath the surface.

2. Combat

Throughout this first phase of Islamic expansion the Muslim armies were ill-equipped and under-manned. In almost all the battles they were fewer in number than the Byzantines. There was, indeed, a difference of three to one in the decisive battle of Yarmuk. They had a small cavalry, the horse being a rare asset in Arabia, they depended on camels, which were much slower and not suited to much of the terrain of al-Sham. The infantry was not only poorly equipped but also inexperienced. In all respects, the lances, arrows, spears and body armour of the Muslims were of inferior quality to the equipment of the Byzantines.

It must be acknowledged, that initially the Byzantines treated the Muslims with contempt and may have considered them an insignificant assortment of bandits in search of worldly gains, who would inevitably be defeated in battle or be easily bought off. However, after Ajnadayn in 634, Heraclius himself appears to have awakened from this delusion and begun to play a commander's role in controlling the manoeuvres of the army from his headquarters in Antioch. The failure of the Byzantines was not due to lack of power but a weakness in resolve and the failure to understand their foe. The Byzantines believed and regarded the Muslims first with contempt and then as an 'ordinary enemy', the likes of the Persians who were out for material gain and worldly glory. Hence the great failure of the Byzantines to recruit defectors from the Muslim ranks, by financial inducements at the Battle of Yarmuk and elsewhere.

The Muslims on the other hand were astute, and aware of the social and religious dissension among the Byzantine subjects. Being so aware, they approached individual tribal leaders and civilians directly. They began to make pacts with them, severing the link with their brutal rulers and bringing them under Islamic rule while offering independence to maintain their religion and culture. This, in the circumstances, proved an extremely fruitful policy. For many rural folk and townspeople, Islamic rule was a deliverance from the Byzantine tyranny. This is exemplified by the prayers and well-wishes of the inhabitants of Damascus and other towns when the Muslims had to evacuate under the threat of a Byzantine counter-attack. Michael the Syrian reports these sentiments aptly: 'Seeing the wickedness of the Byzantines, God brought the Children of Ismail from the south to redeem them.' He further states: 'If the Syrians had some misfortunes (at the hands of the Muslims) these were nothing in comparison to the great blessing of their redemption from the harshness and the wickedness of the Byzantines.'[6]

On the battlefield the Byzantines had the experience of hundreds of years in their war manuals, which they employed at Yarmuk. They also had the assistance of the confederates who had earlier assisted the empire in checking the Persians. In particular the Ghassānids must have fought hard as the battle was being waged on their territory.

Given the numerical and strategic superiority of the Byzantines, the Muslims' victory is all the more remarkable. The Byzantine commitment waned due to several factors. The baggage of several hundred years of association with the empire was beginning to weigh heavy and the Muslims introduced an opportunity for change to some of the confederates. As the Byzantine confederates came to know of the Muslims' equitable, just and fair dealings, their attachment to the Byzantines weakened. The Byzantines, unlike the Muslims viewed death on the battlefield as a loss, whereas the Muslims viewed death as martyrdom and the ultimate victory. No doubt the Muslims' valour and enterprise were far greater and instrumental in gaining their victory.

3. Equitable Policies

Islam changed Arabs from marauding tribes into the most effective agents of liberating civilization. It was their equitable policies, which were in accordance with the Qur'ān and the *Sunna*, that played the greatest role in winning the hearts and minds of the people they came into contact with. Islam revolutionised the social, economic, legal, military, pluralist and feminist philosophies of the time. So much so that over fourteen hundred years later the children of those who first met the pious Muslims have maintained the faith of their liberators.

Unlike any other conquerors in history, the Muslims in battle were made to respect not only their opponents but also their beliefs, their religious symbols and the natural environment. Mutilation and wanton destruction were abhorred and solemn dictates were passed and punishments enforced on anyone who deviated from these commands. Islam changed the conduct of warfare. The looting and pillaging ways of the Byzantines, Persians, and indeed general warfare at the time were abhorrent to Islamic values and therefore abolished. This was in marked contrast to Heraclius' conduct after he defeated the Persians. Muslim warriors were trained to respect every living thing, either from the animal or plant kingdom:

> *Fight in the cause of Allah, those who fight you, but do not transgress the limits: for Allah loves not transgressors.* (al-Baqara 2: 190)

The Prophet ﷺ further clarified the reformed process of warfare, he instructed:

> Set out for *jihād* in the name of Allah and for the sake of Allah. Do not lay hands on the old verging to death, on women, children and babies. Do not steal anything from

> the booty and collect together all that falls to your lot in the battlefield and do good, for Allah loves the virtuous and the pious.[7]

A military strategy that was non-destructive and liberating for the majority emerged from the teachings of Islam. Muslims were repeatedly instructed to only confront those who posed a threat to Islam and did not submit to the conditions laid out for peace under Islamic rule.

The Prophet Muḥammad ﷺ gave this guidance:

> When you meet your enemies who are polytheists, invite them to three courses of action. If they respond to any of these, you also accept them and withhold yourself from doing them any harm. Invite them to (accept) Islam. If they respond to you, accept it from them and desist from fighting against them. Then invite them to migrate from their lands to the land of Muhājirs (the idea was to provide them the opportunity to live in Madina, the stronghold of Islam, so that they may acquire knowledge of Islam and learn its practices) and inform them that, if they refuse to migrate, tell them that they will have the status of Bedouin Muslims and will be subjected to the commands of Allah like other Muslims, but they will not get any share from the spoils of war, except when they actually fight with the Muslims. If they refuse to accept Islam, demand from them the *jizya*. If they agree to pay, accept it from them and hold off your hands. If they refuse to pay the *jizya*, seek Allah's help and fight them.[8]

Thus, war was only conducted as a last resort.

> *But if the enemy incline towards peace, incline towards peace and put your trust in Allah: for He is the One who hears and knows (all things).* (al-Anfāl 8: 61)

Abū Ḥanīfa, one of the greatest Muslim jurists further states: 'If the imām (leader) makes peace with the non-Muslims, or with any particular tribe or body of people, and perceives it to be permissible for the Muslims, there need be no hesitation.'

A point that needs emphasis is that Muslims abhorred conversion by force. The Qur'ān and the *aḥādīth* are very explicit and definite about this:

> *Let there be no compulsion in religion. Truth stands out clear from error...* (al-Baqara 2: 256)
>
> *To you your way of life* (dīn) *and to me mine.* (al-Kāfirūn 109: 6)
>
> *And strive in His cause as you ought to strive (with sincerity and under discipline). He has chosen you, and has imposed no difficulties on you in religion...* (al-Ḥajj 22: 78)

It is to the great credit of Islam that no individual is forced to profess Islam as his faith. Yet Islamic rule must be established by the organized effort and striving of Muslims. In present times this distinction between Islamic rule and Islamic faith has become rather blurred if not totally lost. Those who make rule and faith synonymous paint a picture of Islam as a dictatorial religion. In reality, however, Muslims are urged to fight any injustice and indecency they encounter but not to force anyone to embrace the faith. A person's reward depends upon intention based on the freewill of that person to please his Creator, Allah, and this would become meaningless if induced by force.

The Prophet ﷺ has emphasised: whoever from among you sees a wrong, he must change it by his hands; if he cannot, he must do so by his tongue; if he cannot, he must do so by his heart (through disapproval), but this last would testify to the extreme weakness of faith.[9]

During the epoch of the Prophet ﷺ and the *Khulafā' al-Rāshidūn*, there was a consistent endeavour to preach Islam through liberty. Wherever Muslims attained the upper hand and authority, they compelled nobody to embrace Islam; they tolerated non-Muslims, whether Christians, Jews or Zoroastrians, and further provided the weak in their communities with welfare services.

In the *Hidāya*, the great jurist, Abū Ḥanīfa says: 'It is not lawful to make war upon any people who have never before been called to the faith without previously requiring them to embrace it. The Prophet ﷺ so instructed his commanders, directing them to "Call the non-believers to the faith," and also, because the people will henceforth perceive that they are attacked for the sake of religion, and not for the sake of taking their property, or making slaves of them. On this consideration, it is possible that they may be induced to agree to the call in order to save themselves from the troubles of war.'

This point of the true purpose of war cannot be over-stated. Muslims must only wage war for the advancement of faith and not for any worldly gain. Once a man came to the Prophet ﷺ and asked: 'A man fights for war booty, another fights for fame and a third fights for showing off. Which of them fights Allah's cause?' The Prophet ﷺ said, 'He who fights that Allah's word (i.e. Islam) should be superior, fights in Allah's cause.'[10]

The property of the people of al-Sham was safe and remained in their own custody. The Muslims at no time in the occupation of al-Sham engaged in ethnic cleansing. The land of the occupied territories remained with its original inhabitants and Muslims were restricted from occupying, and initially even from purchasing, this land. In the initial stages there arose a controversy, among the Muslims, when the army requested the possession of occupied land. However, ʿUmar ؓ disagreed, and in a *shūrā* (consultative) meeting he referred to the Qur'ān, *Sūra al-Ḥashr* (59:8–10) *'Some part is due to Muhājirs... and those before them... and those who came after.'* On the basis of these verses, he restricted possession of the conquered lands by private individuals.

ʿUmar is also quoted by al-Bukhārī on the authority of Aslam as saying, 'Were it not for those Muslims who have not come into existence yet, I would have distributed (the land of) every town I conquered among the fighters as the Prophet distributed the land of Khaybar.'

Thus, in the case of al-Sham, the conquered land became public property. The former imperial estates in the possession of Byzantine officers were handed back to the natives of the country. This act alone was a truly revolutionary and liberating episode for the Syrians. It was the first time in their history that they became independent of landlords and free to enjoy the fruits of their labour.

This is in contrast with the sixth – and seventh – century Byzantine, when land ownership was mainly in the hands of the state, or its officers, who permitted the subjects to cultivate it only on the harshest conditions.

The state, in return expected revenue from the subjects in the form of fixed taxes. It was also common for the emperor to reward faithful officers with large estates, giving them a free hand to work the labourers as they wished. This was a major cause of resentment among the poor. There was also other significant land ownership in the hands of the farmer-soldier, and a very limited amount of land was in the form of free peasant holdings. However, the free peasant farmers had to endure stringent taxes, in addition to providing the military with recruits.[11] Moreover, the general legal regime was such that the emperor could evict owners, or tenants without due process, and confiscate or re-allocate their holdings.[12]

Against this, the Muslims made every effort to build up with their subjects relationships founded on trust and fairness without reprisal. Peasant farmers felt free enough to lodge complaints against the Muslim army to the Caliph ʿUmar. A

Christian farmer from al-Sham complained that the Muslim army had marched through his farm and in the process destroyed his crops. ʿUmar ﷺ compensated him for his loss with ten thousand dirhams.[13]

The *kharāj* or land tax, was collected in a just manner and the ability to pay taken into consideration. In a state document relating to al-Ḥīra, in Iraq, the commander Khālid ibn al-Walīd ﷺ reports to the Caliph: 'I counted the male population. They were seven thousand. On further examination, I found one thousand of them were permanently sick and invalid. So I excluded them from the imposition of the *jizya* and those liable to the tax remained six thousand...I have granted them that any old man who can no longer earn his livelihood because of his weaknesses, or who is otherwise afflicted by a calamity, or one has been rich but become so poor as to be dependent on the charity of his co-religionists, I shall exonerate him from the *jizya* and he and his family will be supported by the Muslim Treasury so long as he lives in the Islamic territory...'[14]

The *jizya* once collected from a community became a binding obligation upon the Muslims to safeguard their subjects. When they had to evacuate Emesa, Damascus and other cities in order to check the Byzantines at Yarmuk, the Muslims returned all the tax collected back to their rightful owners because they no longer considered themselves able to honour the contract. Episodes of this nature are unparalleled in history, and totally alien to the confederates of the Byzantines. This example of integration and fairness was very effective in winning over the people.

The main source of taxable income in the Byzantine Empire came from the landowners. The Byzantine law also considered payment of taxes as the primary duty of the peasants. Tax was also levied on crafts, trades, manufacture, retail, export, import, and property (for city dwellers). The variety of levies on such disparate items as recruits and wheat was meant to finance civil and military administration of the empire.

There were two types of tax collectors up to the end of the seventh century. One was the group of public servants known as *decurions*. These collected revenues for the state and were remunerated by the state. The other, called *syntheliai*, consisted of independent tax collectors who raised the fiscal revenue of a province after bidding for the concession at auction. They were obliged to match their bid; if they failed, they were required to make up any shortfall from their own funds.[15] This led many *syntheliai* to resort to severe extortion to obtain taxes from the subjects; some who failed to raise the required taxation they had bid would covertly flee the country. There was a further tax imposed on the village as a separate but collective entity. Indeed, if any village defaulted in payment, its neighbours were obliged to make up the deficit.

The situation in the seventh century was not far from that of Libanius, who was born in 314, in Antioch. He left a very useful diary, in which he mentions villages deserted because of the heavy burden of taxes. 'Tissamenes, the Consular of 386, forced the taxpayers to pay the whole year's tax by the end of the fourth month. A number of persons, both councillors who were collecting the tax and ordinary taxpayers, received beatings from the Consul's soldiers.'[16]

Individual farmers were virtually slaves of the farm owners. In order to prevent farm workers from fleeing their duties and taxes, the following selection from the Theodosian Code illustrates something of the legal status of the farm worker.[17]

'Any person in whose possession a colonus (sharecropper) that belongs to another is found, not only shall restore the aforesaid colonus to his birth status but also shall assume the capitation tax for this man for the time that he was with him.

'Coloni who mediate flight must also be bound with chains and reduced to a servile condition, so that by virtue of their condemnation to slavery, they shall be compelled to fulfil the duties that befit them.

'If any person through solicitation should receive a colonus belonging to another or by concealment should harbour him, he shall be compelled to pay six ounces of gold for him if he is a colonus belonging to a private person and a pound of gold if he is a colonus belonging to an imperial patrimonial estate.'

The inhabitants of al-Sham, and in particular the merchants, suffered from a double tax burden. Their first tax liability was incurred as importers of goods bought from the Far East and a second burden of tax was imposed when they sold the goods on the European continent.

The life of the unemployed took a turn for the worse after the Persian invasion in the early seventh century when the free distribution of bread and assistance from the state ceased. The poor and unemployed were reduced to begging and took to the streets, many without homes or shelter. Their chief concern was to find their next meal.

The privileged classes meanwhile, enjoyed a luxurious lifestyle. They were made up of ex-officials, councillors, lawyers and veterans. Other professions included teachers, doctors, bishops and the officers of the state. Their concerns were regarding building houses with balconies,[18] plays and entertainments.

The tradesmen, who were in no way considered affluent, consisted of bakers, greengrocers, silversmiths, goldsmiths, tavern-keepers, barbers, stonemasons, perfumers, metal workers, cobblers, weavers, sellers of cheese, vinegar, figs and wood.[19] They were all liable to pay the oppressive traders' tax, the 'collatio lustralis'. The tradesmen were legally classified as the underprivileged section of the population; as a result, if they defaulted in tax payment they could be flogged, tortured and even put to death. They might be thrown to the beasts, burnt alive, condemned to a life of hard labour in the mines.[20] The 'traders' tax' was assessed on the capital involved in a business and collected every fifth year[21] to furnish gold for the donations made by the Emperor to the army. The formula used to assess the tax imposed a crushing burden on the small trader, who might even be forced to sell his children into slavery to satisfy the collectors.[22]

No doubt these inequities in taxation and fiscal policy played a role in attracting the Byzantine confederates towards the Muslims and Islamic authority.

The Islamic social security system, which began from the time of Abū Bakr ﷺ was institutionalized during ʿUmar's Caliphate. Once ʿUmar ﷺ was walking along a street, when he encountered a beggar. ʿUmar ﷺ enquired: '...What has constrained you to the state I see you in?' He replied, 'I have to pay the *jizya*, I am poor and old.' Hearing this, ʿUmar ﷺ escorted him by the hand to his own house and gave him something from his private coffers. Then he sent word to the cashier of the *Bayt al-Māl*: 'Look at him and his like. By Allah! We should never be doing justice if we consume his youth and leave him deserted in old age. The government taxes are meant for the poor and the indigent:

> *Alms are for the poor and the needy, and those employed to administer the (funds); for those whose hearts have been (recently) reconciled (to the truth); for those in bondage and in debt, in the cause of Allah; and the wayfarer...* (al-Tawba 9: 60)

This reform of the state's responsibility to the poor and the weak, practised throughout the conquered territories, brought considerable relief to the inhabitants of al-Sham.

Further, Islam's pluralist approach, giving freedom to the people to retain their religion, language, customs and even judicial powers within their own communities added to the appeal of Islamic rule. In *Bible Orient* a Nestorian priest's letter to his friend is quoted: 'These Tayites (Arabs), whom God has accorded domination in these days, have also become our masters, but they do not combat the Christian religion at all. On the other hand they protect our faith, respect our priests and saints and make donations to our churches and our convents.'[23]

The fair and humane treatment of non-Muslim subjects was constantly in the forefront of the Prophet Muḥammad's ﷺ mind. He has quite emphatically said: 'Whoever oppresses a non-Muslim subject or taxes him beyond his capacity, then I shall be the opposite party to him in the litigation.'[24] As for ʿUmar ﷺ, even on his deathbed he exhorted the Companions: 'I exhort you regarding the treatment to be meted out to the people protected by the Messenger of Allah ﷺ (i.e. non-Muslim subjects). They should receive the fullest execution of their covenant and their life and property should be defended even by going to war and they should not be taxed beyond their capacity.'[25]

A non-Muslim was given equal civil rights and he could even file a case against a Muslim. Historical records show that if a Muslim unjustly killed a non-Muslim then the Muslim was slain; if a Muslim wronged a non-Muslim in any way then the law was enforced as merited.

On the whole, the non-Muslims enjoyed vastly greater freedom under Muslim rule than under Byzantine rule. They had the freedom of religious faith and practice. They were exempt from military conscription, whereas the Muslim had a compulsory military duty and service. Their life and property were protected by the state. In sickness and poverty the non-Muslims were not only exempted from the *jizya* but afforded social security benefits. They could file damages and law suits against any Muslim who harmed them. Regarding personal law they were free to adjudicate with reference to their religious belief by their own co-religionists. All of these in return for the payment by those who were liable of the *jizya* and the *kharāj*, which in most cases amounted to less than the *zakāh* which the Muslims had to pay.

Above and beyond the social, legal, economic and religious reforms, Islam introduced to the former confederates of Byzantium, a society of people who had been disciplined in sincerity, equity, morality and God-consciousness by the Prophet Muḥammad ﷺ, who was himself the pinnacle of human excellence in all walks of life. The elite of the Companions of the Prophet ﷺ who advanced into al-Sham were Islam embodied. They demonstrated the excellent qualities commanded by the Prophet's counsel and the Qur'ān. It was the practise of these virtues that opened the way into the hearts of peoples, and not the sword, as the old Western caricature maintained.

NOTES

1. Abdallah el-Khatib, *British Journal of Middle Eastern Studies*, Vol. 28, No. 1, May 2001, p. 30.
2. There is a slight variation in wording in the different narrations. Some state 'Byzantines' while others 'Ghassānids', the confederates of the Byzantines. Either way it indicates Muslim fear of a possible attack on Madina by the Byzantines.
3. Courbage, Youssef and Fargues, Philippe, *Christians and Jews Under Islam*. Trans. Judy Mabro (London, 1997).
4. Abū Bakr ؓ was allocated 6,000 dirhams per annum from the Public Treasury. Just before his death he instructed that part of his land be sold off to raise that amount of money. This was done and the full amount of his drawings was reimbursed to the Public Treasury.
5. Maulānā Muḥammad Yūsuf Kāndhlawī, *Ḥayātus Ṣaḥāba, The Lives of the Companions of the Prophet* (New Delhi, 1987), Vol. 2, p. 325.
6. Michael the Syrian II, from Stratos A. N., *Byzantium in the Seventh Century*, Vol. I, pp. 602-634. Trans. Marc Ogilvie Grant (Amsterdam, 1968), Vol. II, p. 129.
7. *Ṣaḥīḥ* Muslim, *Ḥadīth* 5958, Vol. 4, p. 1294, trans. Abdul Hamid Siddiqi, *Kitāb Bhavan*, New Delhi, India, 1987.
8. Ibid.
9. Ibid.

10. Bukhārī, *Ṣaḥīḥ al-Bukhārī*, Trans. Dr. Muhammad Muhsin Khan. (Lahore, Kazi Publications, 1984. In *Ṣaḥīḥ* Muslim a similar narration is concluded '... who fights that the word of Allah be exalted, fights in the way of Allah.'
11. Geanakoplos, Deno John, *Byzantium – Church, Society and Civilisation seen through contemporary eyes* (Chicago 1984), p. 231.
12. Kazhdan and Constable, *People and Power in Byzantium* (Washington, DC, Dumbarton Oaks, 1982), p. 145.
13. Nuʿmānī, Shiblī, *Al-Farūq: Bayhaqī and Jāḥiẓ* (Delhi, Imad Publications, 1987), p. 254.
14. Hamidullah, Muhammad, *The Muslim Conduct of State* (Lahore, Sh. Muhammad Ashraf, 1942), p. 202.
15. Geanakoplos, Deno John, op. cit., p. 234.
16. Liebeschuetz, J. H.W. G., *Antioch – city and imperial administration in the later Roman Empire* (Oxford, Clarendon Press, 1972), p. 164.
17. Geanakoplos, Deno John, op. cit., p. 229.
18. Ibid., p. 261.
19. Liebeschuetz, op. cit., p. 52.
20. Ibid.
21. The fiscal policies varied slightly with successive Emperors; however the burden was always heavy on the poor.
22. From Liebeschuetz, op. cit., p. 54. [Also for more details see J. R. Palanque and P.de Labriolle, *The Church in the Christian Roman Empire.* Trans. E. C. Messenger (London, 1952).]
23. Hamidullah, Muhammad, op. cit. From Assemani, *Bible Orient*, III, 2, p. xcvi; De Goeje, *Memoire sur la conquete de la Syrie*, p. 106.
24. Bukhari, *Ṣaḥīḥ al-Bukhārī*, Trans. Dr. Muhammad Muhsin Khan. (Lahore, Kazi Publications, 1984
25. Nuʿmānī, Shiblī, op. cit., p. 338.

Appendix A

Rulers

ISLAMIC WORLD

The Prophet Muḥammad ﷺ	612 - 632
Khulafā' al-Rā'shidūn	
(The rightly-guided Caliphs)	632 - 661
Abū Bakr ؓ	632 - 634
ʿUmar ؓ	634 - 644
ʿUthmān ؓ	644 - 656
ʿAlī ؓ	656 - 661

BYZANTINE EMPERORS

Constantine I	324 - 337
Constantius	337 - 361
Julian	361 - 363
Jovian	363 - 364
Valens	364 - 378
Theodosius I	379 - 395
Arcadius	395 - 408
Theodosius II	408 - 450
Marcian	450 - 457
Leo I	457 - 474

Leo II	474
Zeno	474 - 475
Basilicus	475 - 476
Zeno (2nd time)	476 - 491
Anastasius I	491 - 518
Justin I	518 - 527
Justinian I	527 - 565
Justin II	565 - 578
Tiberius I	578 - 582
Maurice	582 - 602
Phocas	602 - 610
Heraclius	610 - 641
Heraclonas	641
Constans II	641 - 668

PERSIAN EMPERORS

Chosroes II (Parviz)	590 - 628
Kavad II (Siroes)	628
Ardaser III	628 - 629
Sarbaros (Sarbarazas)	629
Borane	629 - 630
Hormisdas V	630 - 632
Yazdagird III	632 - 651

Appendix B

Months of the Islamic '*Hijra*' Calendar

Muḥarram
Ṣafar
Rabīʿ al-Awwal
Rabīʿ al-Ākhir (also called Rabīʿ al-Thānī)
Jumādā al-Ūlā
Jumādā al-Ākhira (also called Jumādā al-Thānī)
Rajab
Shaʿbān
Ramaḍān
Shawwāl
Dhū al-Qaʿda
Dhū al-Ḥijja

The Islamic calendar began with the *Hijra* (migration) of the Messenger of Allah, Muḥammad ﷺ from Makka to Madina on 16 July 622, thus corresponding with 1 Muḥarram 1 AH. AH denotes *Anno Hijre*. The Islamic calendar is a religious calendar based upon the moon's orbit.

Appendix C

Chronology of Events

23 May 627 – 10 May 628

Ḥārith ibn ʿUmar ☒ is despatched to Buṣrā, in al-Sham to invite its leader to Islam.
Daḥya al-Kalbī despatched to Heraclius.

1 May 629 – 19 April 630

Battle of Muʼta.
Conquest of Makka.

20 April 630 – 8 April 631

The expedition to Tabuk.

9 April 631 – 28 March 632

Farewell *Ḥajj* of the Prophet ☒.

29 March 632 – 18 March 633

The Prophet ☒ falls ill and passes away.
Abū Bakr ☒ elected as the first Caliph.
Usāma ibn Zayd despatched to al-Sham;
an uprising of apostates and rebels ensues.

18 March 633 – 6 March 634

Khālid ibn Saʿīd ﵁ despatched to al-Sham for a reconnaissance mission.
Khālid ibn al-Walīd ﵁ despatched to Iraq.

7 March 634 – 24 February 635

ʿAmr ibn al-ʿĀṣ ﵁, Abū ʿUbayda ibn Jarrāḥ ﵁, Yazīd ibn Abī Sufyān ﵁, and Shuraḥbīl ibn Ḥasana ﵁ are appointed as commanders of their respective battalions and despatched to al-Sham to confront the Byzantine forces.
Battle of Ajnadayn.
Battle of Fihl.
Abū Bakr passes away.
ʿUmar ibn al-Khaṭṭāb ﵁ appointed the second Caliph.

25 February 635 – 13 February 636

Khālid ﵁ arrives in al-Sham.
The fall of Damascus.
Ḥimṣ.
Baʿlabak.

14 February 636 – 1 February 637

Battle of Yarmuk.
ʿIkrama ibn Abī Jahl ﵁ is martyred at Yarmuk.

2 February 637 – 22 January 638

The liberation of Jerusalem.

Appendix D

Jihād

The word *jihād* is derived from the verb *jāhada,* which means, 'he exerted himself'. This literally means exertion or striving. *Jihād* in its legal and religious sense signifies self-exertion to the utmost of one's capacity in the cause of Allah. This is why *jihād* has been used as the opposite to the word *Quʿūd* (sitting) in the Qur'ān (4: 95). Thus *jihād* in Islam is not an act of violence directed indiscriminately against non-Muslims. It is the name given to an all-round struggle, which a Muslim should undertake against evil in whatever form or shape it appears. As for '*Qitāl fī sabīlillāh*' (physical fighting in the way of Allah), this is only one aspect of *jihād*.[1]

The Qur'an gives this eloquent example of *jihād*:

> *Those who believe, and suffer exile and strive with might and main, in Allah's cause, with their goods and their persons, have the highest rank in the sight of Allah. They are the people who will achieve (salvation).* (al-Tawba 9: 20)

Jihād or *qitāl* is not an individual but a collective obligation, which if discharged by a sufficient number of people, will not bring condemnation on the rest for neglect of that duty.

The practice of the Prophet Muḥammad ﷺ also shows that either he organized the expeditions himself or delegated authority to the responsible governors or tribal chieftains.

The jurist, Abū Yūsuf, the Chief *Qāḍī* (Justice) of the Caliph Hārūn al-Rashīd, says: 'No army marches without the permission of the Caliph (Central Government).'[2]

LEGITIMATE REASONS FOR MUSLIMS TO WAGE WAR

Defensive

> *Fight in the cause of Allah those who fight you but do not transgress limits; for Allah loves not transgressors.* (al-Baqara 2: 190)

That a nation has the right to defend itself from attack needs no great argument. However, even concerning the right to defend one's nation the Qur'ān warns against transgressing the limits.

The need and merit of defensive war was further emphasized by the Prophet Muḥammad ﷺ who said, 'Whoever fights in defence of his person and is killed, he is a martyr; whoever is killed in defence of his property, is a martyr; whoever fights in defence of his family and is killed, is a martyr; and whoever is killed for the cause of Allah, is a martyr.'

Sympathetic

A Muslim nation should be obliged to assist or may even wage war upon another state if the Muslim citizens of that nation request assistance on the grounds that they are being oppressed because of their religious beliefs.

> *Those who believed, and adopted exile, and fought for the faith, with their property and their persons, in the cause of Allah, as well as those who gave (them) asylum and aid – these are all friends and protectors, one of another. As to those who believed*

> *but came not into exile; if they seek your aid in religion, it is your duty to help them, except against a people with whom you have a treaty of mutual alliance. And remember Allah sees all that you do.* (al-Anfāl 8: 72)
>
> *And why should you not fight in the cause of Allah and of those who, being weak, are ill treated (and oppressed)? Men, women and children, whose cry is: 'Our Lord! Rescue us from this town, whose people are oppressors and raise for us from Thee one who will protect; and raise for us from Thee one who will help!'* (al-Nisā' 4: 75)

Punitive

The practical examples of punitive actions stem from the earliest period of Islam. During the period of the Rightly-Guided Caliphs punitive actions were undertaken against apostates, against those who refused to pay *zakāh,* against religious rebels, against those who broke their covenants, against those who formed sub-Islamic groups and considered the main body of Muslims as apostates (e.g. Khārijites).

Apostates

Apostasy in Muslim law means turning away from Islam after being a Muslim. The sayings and deeds of the Prophet ﷺ, and the general consensus of learned Muslims is to prescribe capital punishment for an apostate. To wage war against apostates is justified on the same principles on which the punishment of a solitary apostate is based. Nevertheless, Muslim jurists emphasize that before prosecuting and condemning an apostate, it is necessary to discuss the matter with him and try to remove his doubts regarding the Islamic point of view in the matter concerned. Time must be given to reflect on the problems, sometimes up to several months. Exempted from capital punishment are minors, the insane and those under duress.

Disputes

We first need to discuss disputes between Muslims. As Islam is based on the unity of men and the positive aspects of life, all types of rebellion are forbidden. Yet being a practical religion, the law has been laid down by the Qur'ān thus:

> *If two parties among the believers fall into a quarrel, make peace between them: but if one of them transgresses beyond bounds against the other, then fight against the one that transgresses until he complies, then make peace between them with justice and be fair: for Allah loves those who are fair (and just).* (al-Ḥujurāt 49: 9)

To emphasize the unity of mankind:

> *Mankind! Verily We created you of a male and a female, and We have made you nations and tribes that you might know one another. Verily the noblest of you with Allah is the most pious of you. Verily Allah is the Knowing, the Wise* (al-Ḥujurāt 49: 13)

As to the other categories, Muslims can wage war against 'persons' or communities who resist the Imām's authority and reside in a state of disobedience to the Imām without due cause, whether in open force or otherwise; and those who rob and murder Muslims. Several incidents of rebellion by non-Muslims occurred during the early period of Islam. During the Caliphate of ʿUmar ibn al-Khaṭṭāb ﵁, the Jews of Khaybar incited rebellion against the state and also made constant efforts to harm and kill lone Muslims. At their peak they turned to armed rebellion. ʿUmar ﵁ therefore decided to expel them from the land of the Ḥijāz.[3]

Non-Payment of Zakāh

The much-quoted *ḥadīth* will suffice to illustrate the course of action needed. The Prophet Muḥammad ﷺ has said, 'I have been ordered to fight people until they attest that there is no deity but Allah, and that I am the Messenger of Allah, that they establish prayer and pay the *zakāh*. If they do that, they are saved from my attack on their persons and their buildings, and the reckoning of their affairs lies with Allah.'

Abū Bakr ﷺ during the early days of his Caliphate took action against those who refused to pay the *zakāh*.

Religious opposition

The example of the Khārijites is instructive. The Khārijites were an anarchic group who accused all other Muslims of heresy and even unbelief. If Khārijites do not offer armed resistance to the established government, they may be tolerated as any other orthodox sect. If they are not passive and try to destabilize the government, they should be treated like rebels and confronted.

Idealistic

Islam's ideals place great emphasis on the unity of Allah and the vicegerency of man on earth. This implies that, in the eyes of Allah, all the faithful are equal, irrespective of race, sex, status or power and also that the word of Allah should rule supreme on the earth.

It is this mission to uproot evil and godlessness and replace it with a just, God-conscious being that drives Muslims along the path of Allah in the form of *jihād*. By this we do not mean to go and kill anyone and everyone who refuses to accept Islam, but to set out on a mission to convey Islamic principles and to invite and win over those who wish to do so of their own free-will. The aim and final goal is to try and establish the Islamic code of conduct on earth for the benefit of all mankind.

The Qur'ān has scores of verses on this subject:

> *It is He who has sent His Apostle with guidance and the religion of truth, to proclaim it over all religion, even though the Pagans*

may detest (it). (al-Tawba 9: 33) (See also al-Fatḥ 48: 28 and al-Ṣaff 61: 9.)

You are the best of people evolved for mankind. Enjoining what is right, forbidding what is wrong, and believing in Allah... (Āl ʿImrān 3: 110)

Say: O you that reject faith! I worship not that which you worship. Nor will you worship that which I worship. And I will not worship that which you have been wont to worship. Nor will you worship that which I worship. To you be your way of life (dīn), *and to me mine.* (al-Kāfirūn 109: 1-6)

The Prophet's ﷺ letter to the Emperor clearly indicates the stance Islam takes towards non-Muslim states: The Messenger of Allah ﷺ first invites the Emperor to embrace Islam. He said: 'If (you do) not, pay *jizya*... if not, then (at least) do not interfere with the (Roman) subjects if they embrace Islam or if they offer to pay *jizya*.'[4] Only when all peaceful avenues are exhausted, may forceful measures be adopted.

To reiterate the Prophet's ﷺ saying: 'Whoever among you sees an indecency, he must change it by his hand; if he cannot, he must do so by his tongue; if he cannot, he must do so by his heart (through disapproval) but this last would testify to the extreme weakness of faith.'

It is with these facts about *jihād* in mind that one should seek to understand the Islamic principles of war. This is vital to an understanding of the motivation for the Muslims' advance into al-Sham against the Byzantines.

ACTS FORBIDDEN IN WAR

1. Unnecessary cruelty and torture in killing. The Prophet ﷺ has said, 'Fairness is prescribed by Allah in every matter, so if you kill, kill in a fair way.'

2. Execution of non-combatants. That is people who do not partake in the battle, such as women, minors, servants, slaves who accompany their masters but do not take part in the actual fighting. The blind and physically handicapped, monks, hermits, the very old, the insane and delirious.

3. Decapitation of prisoners of war. Capital punishment of prisoners of war is not desirable. The Prophet ﷺ condemned the beheading of prisoners of war.

4. Mutilation of men as well as beasts.

5. Treachery and/or breach of faith.

6. Devastation, destruction of harvest, and cutting down trees. The Qur'ān ascribes these acts of destruction to the hypocrites and mischief-makers. It states:

> When he (the hypocrite) turns his back, his aim everywhere is to spread mischief through the earth and destroy crops and cattle. But Allah loves not mischief. (al-Baqara 2: 205)

7. Slaughtering animals more than is necessary for food.

8. Excess and wickedness.

9. Adultery and fornication even with captive women.

10. Execution of enemy hostages, even if those of the Muslim state have been murdered by the enemy, and even if there is an express agreement that hostages may be beheaded in retaliation.

11. Decapitation of fallen enemy and sending the head or body to a higher Muslim authority is regarded as improper and disliked (Abū Bakr ؓ issued orders forbidding this).

12. Massacre after the enemy has been defeated.

13. Killing parents even if they are non-Muslims and in the enemy ranks. There are numerous cases when the Prophet ﷺ forbade persons who had asked permission

to kill their non-Muslim parents on account of their hostility to Islam.

14. Execution of peasants when they do not fight and the result of war is of no concern to them.
15. Execution of traders, merchants, contractors and the like if they do not take part in actual fighting.
16. Burning to death a captured man or animal. The Prophet ﷺ has said, 'Only the Lord of Fire can punish with fire.'
17. The use of human shields in the early days of Islam was common for the non-Muslims. There is no incidence in the history of Islamic warfare where such a tactic was employed.

Appendix E

Jizya

The *jizya* can be defined as a tax, which is levied upon subjects of the Muslim state who are of different faiths, but claim protection and social welfare from the Muslim state. In return for the tax, it becomes mandatory on the Muslims to protect the non-Muslims' person and property, their livestock, agricultural produce and lands.

> *Fight those who do not believe in Allah or the Last Day. Who do not hold that forbidden which has been forbidden by Allah and His Messenger; We do not acknowledge the religion of truth (even if they are) of the People of the Book, until they pay the* jizya *with willing submission, and feel themselves subdued.* (al-Tawba 9: 29)

According to Imām Abū Ḥanīfa, founder of the Ḥanafī school of law, *jizya* is of two kinds:[5] that which is established voluntarily, and that which is enforced. The usual rate was one dinar for every adult male. The law exempted females, children, paupers, and old men.[6] He who pays *jizya* to a Muslim state and obtains protection is called a *dhimmī*. It is important to note that the *jizya* in some cases was less than the *zakāh*, which is obligatory on all Muslim men and women. The *jizya* to be portrayed as an oppressive tax has been labelled by some authors as a poll tax, capitation tax, protection tax and so forth. Those who rant about the injustice of Muslim states for the imposition of *jizya* on non-Muslims should reflect on the historical reality, and on the actual contribution to state funds by the *dhimmīs* as compared to the Muslims themselves. Most inhabitants were more than happy to pay the *jizya* to the Muslim state, for not only was it less than the tax imposed by the Byzantines but the *dhimmīs* then enjoyed exemption from military service and had autonomy in personal law. Moreover their lives and property were then protected by the Muslim state. In addition, ability to pay was taken into account, rather than the brutal and blanket approach practised by the Byzantines.

Imām Mālik said: 'The *sunna* is that there is no *jizya* due from women or children of People of the Book, and that *jizya* is only taken from men who have reached puberty. The people of *dhimma* and the magians do not have to pay any *zakāh* on their palms or their vines or their crops or their livestock. This is because *zakāh* is imposed on the Muslims to purify them and to be given back to their poor, whereas *jizya* is imposed on the People of the Book to humble them. As long as they are in the country they have agreed to live in, they do not have to pay anything on their property except the *jizya*. If, however, they trade in Muslim countries, coming and going in them, a tenth is taken from what they invest in such trade. This is because *jizya* is only imposed on them on conditions, which they have agreed on, namely that they will remain in their own countries, and that war will be waged for them on any enemy of theirs, and that if they then leave that land to go anywhere else to do business they will have to pay a tenth. Whoever among them does business with the people of Egypt, and then goes to Syria, and then does business with the people of Syria and then goes to Iraq and does business with them and then goes on to Madina, or Yemen, or other similar places, has to pay a tenth.

'People of the Book and magians do not have to pay any *zakāh* on any of their property, livestock, produce or crops. The *sunna* still continues like that. They remain in the *dīn* they were in, and they continue to do what they used to do. If in any one year they frequently come and go in Muslim countries then they have to pay a tenth every time they do so, since that is outside what they have agreed upon, and not one of the conditions stipulated for them. This is what I have seen the people of knowledge of our city doing.'

It is reported from the Prophet Muḥammad ﷺ that, 'Whoever oppresses a non-Muslim subject or taxes him beyond his capacity, then I shall be the opposite party to him in the litigation.' Further, 'Umar ؓ, the second Caliph, counselled from his deathbed, 'I exhort my successor regarding the treatment to be meted out to the people protected by the Messenger of Allah (i.e. non-Muslim subjects). They should receive the fullest execution of their covenant, and their lives and property should be defended even by going to war, and they should not be taxed beyond their capacity.'

NOTES

1. *Ṣaḥīḥ* Muslim, Trans. Abdul Hamid Siddiqi. (Delhi, Kitab Bhavan, 1979), p. 938.
2. Hamidullah, Muhammad, *The Muslim Conduct of State* (Lahore, Sh. Muhammad Ashraf, 1942), p. 306.
3. See *ḥadīth* in *Ṣaḥīḥ* Muslim, op. cit., p. 965, *Ḥadīth* No. 4366 for more detail.
4. Hamidullah, Muhammad, op. cit.
5. The *Hīdāya* of al-Marghīnānī. Trans. Charles Hamilton, Darul Ishaat, Urdu Bazaar, Karachi, Pakistan, 1989, Vol. II, p. 211.
6. Imām Abū Yūsuf states: '*jizya* is to be imposed on the aged who possess property and excess capital'.

Appendix F

The Story of Kaʿb ibn Mālik

Kaʿb ibn Mālik:

I have never stayed behind when the Prophet went on any expedition, except that of Badr. Neither God nor the Prophet blamed anyone for staying behind at the time of Badr, because the Prophet set out from Madina to intercept a trade caravan which belonged to the Quraysh. The battle took place without any preparation or prior planning. On the other hand, I had attended the pledge of the *Anṣār* to the Prophet at ʿAqabah when we made our commitment to Islam absolutely clear. I would not exchange my attendance there with taking part in the Battle of Badr, although Badr is the more famous occasion.

Nevertheless, I failed to join the army of the expedition of Tabūk. I was never in better circumstances or more physically able than I was then. At no time did I have two means of transport except on that occasion. It was the habit of the Prophet to keep his destination secret. This time, however, setting his destination so far away, and moving in an exceptionally hot climate, he made it clear to the people that he intended to attack the Byzantines. Those who joined the Prophet were in such large numbers that no register of them could have been kept.

In the circumstances, anyone who wished to stay behind might have thought that he would not be noticed, unless God chose to inform the Prophet about him by revelation. The Prophet decided to launch that attack at a time when fruits were abundant and people preferred to stay in the shade. The Prophet and the Muslims, however, were busy getting ready for their impending task. I went out day after day to the marketplace in order to get my equipment, but I always came back having done nothing. I always thought that I was able to get whatever I needed in no time. Nevertheless, I continued in that condition until it was time to move. The Prophet and the army with him started their march and I had not got my preparations under way. I thought to myself: 'I can still get myself ready in a day or two and should be able to catch up with them.' When they had covered quite a distance, I went out to the market and came back having done nothing. This continued day after day. By this time, the army must have covered quite a long distance. I thought I must make a move now and catch up with them. I wish I had done that, but I did not. Every time I went out after the Prophet and the army had left, I was troubled by the fact that I saw only people who were known to be hypocrites or people who were physically unable to join the army. My place was not with either group. I was told that the Prophet did not mention me until he had arrived at Tabūk. He remarked once to those who were present at Tabūk: 'What has happened to Kaʿb ibn Mālik?' A man from the tribe of Salamah said to him: 'Messenger of God, his wealth and arrogance made him stay behind.' Muʿādh ibn Jabal said to him: 'What a foul remark! Messenger of God, we have known nothing bad of the man.' The Prophet made no comment.

I soon heard that the Prophet and his Companions had started on their journey back from Tabūk. I felt very sad. To tell a lie was paramount in my mind. I started thinking about what to say to the Prophet tomorrow, after his arrival, in order to spare myself his anger. I sought the help of everyone in my household. When it was mentioned that the Prophet was soon to arrive, all thoughts of seeking a false excuse disappeared from my mind. I realized that the only way to spare myself the Prophet's anger was to tell the truth. I was determined, therefore, to say exactly what happened.

The Prophet then arrived in Madinah. It was his habit when he came back from travelling to go first to the mosque and pray two *rakʿahs* before sitting to meet the people. When he did that, those who had stayed behind went to him and stated their excuses, swearing to their truth. They were over 80 people. The Prophet accepted their statements and oaths and prayed to God to forgive them, leaving it to God to judge them by His knowledge. I then followed and greeted the Prophet. He met my greeting with an angry smile. He then told me to come forward. I went to him and sat down facing him. He said, 'What caused you to stay behind? Have you not bought your transport?'

I said to him, 'Messenger of God, had I been speaking to anyone on the face of the earth other than you, I would have been able to avoid his anger by giving some sort of an excuse. I can make a case for myself. But I know for certain that if I were to tell you lies in order to win your pleasure, God would soon make the truth known to you and I would incur your displeasure. If, on the other hand, I tell you the truth and you are not happy with me because of it, I would hope for a better result from God. By God, I have no excuse whatsoever. I have never been more physically able or in better circumstances than I was when I stayed behind.' The Prophet said to me: 'You have certainly said the truth. You await God's judgement.'

After I left, some men from the clan of Salamah followed me and said: 'We have never known you to commit a sin before this. You could certainly have given the Prophet an excuse like all those who stayed behind. You would have been spared this trouble had the Prophet prayed to God to forgive you, as he would surely have done.' They continued pressing me on this to the extent that I wished to go back to the Prophet and tell him that I was lying. Before I did that, however, I asked whether anyone else said the same thing as I did. They replied that two more people said the same and were given the same answer. When I asked their names, they mentioned Murārah ibn al-Rabīʿ and Hilāl ibn Umayyah. I knew these two to be men of faith and sincere devotion. I realized that the proper attitude for me was to be in their company. I therefore made no further move.

The Prophet ordered all his Companions not to speak to us three. He made no similar instruction concerning anybody else of those who stayed behind. All people were now evading us. Their attitude was changed. It was very hard for me that I did not even know myself or the place I was in. This was no longer the town I lived in. My world had changed. We continued in this condition for 50 days.

My two Companions, Murārah ibn al-Rabīʿ and Hilāl ibn Umayyah, stayed at home. I was the youngest of the three. I continued to go out and attend the congregational prayers with other Muslims. I frequented all the markets, but nobody would speak to me. I would also go to the Prophet and greet him as he sat down after prayers. I would always think to myself: 'Have I detected any movement on his lips suggesting that he has answered my greeting?' I would pray close to him and look at him stealthily. When I was preoccupied with my prayers, he would look at me, but when I looked towards him, he would turn his face the other way.

When this boycott by all the Muslim community seemed to have lasted too long, I climbed the wall of an orchard which belonged to a cousin of mine named Abū Qatādah, who was very close to me. I greeted him, but he did not answer. I said to him: 'Abū Qatādah, I beseech you by God to answer me: do you know that I love God and His Messenger?' He did not answer. I repeated my question three times, but he still did not answer.

I then beseeched him once again, and his answer came: 'God and His Messenger know better.' Tears sprang to my eyes and I came down. I went to the market and as I was walking I saw a man, apparently a stranger from Syria, enquiring about me. People pointed me out to him. He came to me and handed me a letter from the King of Ghassān, the Arab tribe in Syria. The letter was written on a piece of silk and read: 'We have learnt that your friend has imposed a boycott on you. God has not placed you in a position of humiliation. If you join us, we will endeavour to alleviate all your troubles.' When I read it, I thought it to be yet another test of my sincerity. I have reached so low that an unbeliever hopes that I would willingly join him. I put the letter in an oven and burnt it.

When we had spent 40 nights in that situation, a messenger from the Prophet came to me and said: 'God's Messenger (peace be upon him) commands you to stay away from your wife.' I asked whether that meant that I should divorce her and he answered in the negative. He told me only to stay away from her. My two Companions also received the same instruction. I told my wife to go to her people's home and stay there until God had given His judgement in this matter.

Hilāl ibn Umayyah was an old man. His wife went to the Prophet and said, 'Messenger of God, Hilāl ibn Umayyah is very old and has no servant. Do you mind if I continue to look after him?' He said, 'That is all right, but do not let him come near you.' She said, 'By God, these things are far from his mind. He has not stopped crying ever since this has happened to him. I indeed fear for his eyesight.' Some people in my family suggested that I should seek the Prophet's permission to let my wife look after me. I said, 'I am not going to ask him that. I do not know what his answer would be, considering that I am a young man.'

Another ten nights passed, to complete 50 nights since the Prophet instructed the Muslims not to talk to us. At dawn after the 50th night I prayed at the top of one of our houses. I was still in that condition which I have described: the world seemed to me suffocatingly small and I did not recognize myself any more. As I sat down after the dawn prayers, however, I heard a voice from the direction of Mount Salʿ saying: 'Kaʿb ibn Mālik! Rejoice!' I realized that my hardship was over, and I prostrated myself in gratitude to God.

What happened was that the Prophet informed the congregation after finishing the dawn prayer that God has pardoned us. People moved fast to give us that happy news. A man came at speed on horseback to bring me the news, while another from the tribe of Aslam went on top of the mountain to shout it to me. His voice was quicker than the horse. When I heard that man's voice giving me the happiest piece of news I ever received, I gave him my two garments as a gesture of gratitude. By God, they were the only clothes I had at the time. I borrowed two garments and went quickly to the Prophet. People were meeting me in groups, saying, 'Congratulations on being forgiven by God.' I entered the mosque and saw the Prophet sitting with a group of people around him. Ṭalḥah ibn ʿUbaydullāh came quickly towards me, shook my hand and congratulated me. He was the only one from the *Muhājirīn* to do that. I will never forget Ṭalḥah's kindness.

When I greeted the Prophet, he said to me, with his face beaming with pleasure, 'Rejoice, for this is your happiest day since you were born!' I asked him: 'Is my pardon from you, Messenger of God, or is it from God?' He said, 'It is from God.' When the Prophet was pleased at something, his face would light up and look like the moon. We always recognized that.

When I sat down facing him, I said to him, 'Messenger of God, I will make my repentance complete by giving away all my property in charity.' The Prophet said, 'Keep some of your property, for that is better for you.' I answered that I would keep my share in Khaybar. I then added that I was forgiven only because I told the truth, and I would make my repentance complete by never telling a lie at any time in my life.

I feel that the greatest grace God has bestowed on me ever since He guided me to accept Islam is my telling the truth to the Prophet on that day. Had I invented some false excuse, I would have perished like all those who told him lies. God has described those people in the worst description ever. He says in the Qur'ān: '*When you return to them they will swear to you by God so that you may let them be. Let them be, then: they are unclean. Hell shall be their abode in recompense for what they used to do. They swear to you trying to make you pleased with them. Should you be pleased with them, God shall never be pleased with such transgressing folk.*' (Verses 95–96) I have never knowingly or deliberately told a lie ever since I said that to the Prophet. I pray to God to help me keep my word for the rest of my life.[1]

NOTE

1. Sayyid Quṭb, *In The Shade of the Qur'ān: Fī Ẓilāl al-Qur'ān*, Vol. VIII, The Islamic Foundation, Leicester, 2003, pp. 288-293.

Bibliography

TRANSLATIONS OF THE QUR'ĀN

Ali, A. Yusuf, *The Holy Qur'ān* (Islamic Propagation Centre International, 1946)

Shafi', Maulānā Muftī Muḥammad, *Ma'āriful Qur'ān.* Trans. Prof. Muhammad Hasan Askari and Prof. Muhammad Shamim. Revised by Justice Muti Muhammad Taqi Usmani. (Karachi, Maktaba-e-Darul Uloom Karachi, 1996)

'Usmānī, 'Allama Shabbīr, *The Holy Qur'ān.* Trans. Muhammad Ashfaq Ahmad. (New Delhi, Idara Isha'at-E-Diniyat, 1992)

AḤĀDĪTH

Abū Dāwūd. *Sunan Abī Dāwūd.* Trans. Prof. Ahmad Hassan. (Lahore, Sh. Muhammad Ashraf, 1984)

Abū Muḥammad al-Ḥusain ibn Mas'ūd Muḥammad al-Farrā' (or Ibn al-Farrā') al-Baghawī. Revised by Walī ad-Dīn Muḥammad ibn 'Abdallāh al-Khaṭīb at-Tibrīzī, *Mishkāt al-Maṣābīḥ.* Trans. Dr. James Robson. (Lahore, Sh. Muhammad Ashraf, 1994)

Bukhārī, Imām, *Ṣaḥīḥ al-Bukhārī.* Trans. Dr. Muhammad Muhsin Khan. (Lahore, Kazi Publications, 1984)

Muslim, Imām, *Ṣaḥīḥ* Muslim. Trans. Abdul Hamid Siddiqi. (Delhi, Kitab Bhavan, 1979)

Mālik, Imām ibn Anas, *Al-Muwaṭṭa'*. Trans. Aisha Abdurrahman Bewley. (Granada, Spain, Madinah Press Granada, 1989)

Al-Nawawī, Imām, *Riyāḍ al-Ṣāliḥīn*. Trans. S. M. Madni Abbasi. (Karachi, International Islamic Publishers, 1991)

Tirmidhī, Imām, *Sunan al-Tirmidhī*. (Urdu Version). (Karachi, Idara Ishā'at, 1985)

CLASSICAL ARABIC SOURCES

Balādhurī, al-Imām abū'l-'Abbās Aḥmad ibn Jābir, *Kitāb Futūḥ Al-Buldān, The Origins of the Islamic State*. Trans. Phillip Khuri Hitti. (Beirut, Khayats, 1966)

Ibn Isḥāq, *Sīrat Rasūl Allāh, The Life of Muhammad*. Trans. A. Guillaume. (Karachi, Oxford Uni. Press, 1967)

Shaybānī, Muḥammad. *Kitābus-Siyar* 'The Islamic Law of Nations'. Trans. Majid Khadduri. (School of Advanced Int. Studies, Johns Hopkins Uni., 1965)

Suyūtī, Jalāl ad-Dīn, *The History of The Caliphs*. Trans. Major H. S. Jarrett. (Karachi, Karimsons, 1980)

———, *Ta'rīkh al-Khulafā', The History of the Caliphs Who Took The Right Way*. Trans. Abdassamad Clarke. (London, Ta-Ha, 1996)

al-Ṭabarī, *Ta'rīkh al-Ṭabarī, The History of al-Ṭabarī*, Vol. IX, 'The Last Years of the Prophet'. Trans. Ismail K. Poonawala. (Albany, State Uni. of New York, 1990)

———, *Ta'rīkh al-Ṭabarī, The History of al-Ṭabarī*, Vol. X, 'The Conquest of Arabia', Trans. Fred M. Donner. (Albany, State Uni. of New York, 1993)

———, *Ta'rīkh al-Ṭabarī, The History of al-Ṭabarī*, Vol. XI, 'The Challenge to the Empires'. Trans. Khalid Yahya Blankinship. (Albany, State Uni. of New York, 1993)

———, *Ta'rīkh al-Ṭabarī, The History of al-Ṭabarī*, Vol. XII, 'The Battle of al-Qadisiyah and the Conquest of al-Sham and Palestine'. Trans. Yohanan Friedmann. (Albany, State Uni. of New York, 1992) al-Ṭabarī, *Ta'rīkh al-Ṭabarī, The History of al-Ṭabarī*, Vol. XIII, 'The Conquest of Iraq, southwestern Persia and Egypt'. Trans. Gautier H.A. Juynboll. (Albany, State University of New York, 1989)

Al-Wāqidī, Muḥammad ibn ʿUmar, *Kitāb al-Maghāzī*. Trans. Marsden Jones, Vols. I, II and III. (Oxford, Oxford Uni. Press, 1966)

GREEK AND SYRIAN SOURCES

Nikephoros, *Nikephoros Patriarch of Constantinople, Short History*. Trans. Cyril Mango. (Washington, Dumbarton Oaks, 1990)

Paschale, *Chronicon Paschale 284-628 AD*. Trans, Michael Whitby and Mary Whitby. (Liverpool, Liverpool Uni. Press, 1989)

Pseudo-Dionysius of Tel-Mahre, *Chronicle Part III*. Trans. Witold Witakowski. (Liverpool, Liverpool Uni. Press, 1996)

The Armenian History attributed to Sebeos. Trans. R.W. Thomson. Historica; Comm. by James Howard-Johnston. (Liverpool, Liverpool Uni. Press, 1999)

The Seventh Century in West-Syrian Chronicles. Trans. Andrew Palmer. (Liverpool, Liverpool Uni. Press, 1993)

Theophanes, *The Chronicles of Theophanes*. Trans. Harry Turtledove. (Philadelphia, Uni. of Pensylvania Press, 1982)

OTHER SOURCES

Ahmad, Fazal, *Omar, the Second Caliph of Islam*. (Delhi, Idara Ishāʿat-E-Diniyat, n.d.)

Arnold, Sir Thomas, *The Caliphate*. (Delhi, Adam Publishers, 1992)

Al-Aṣfahānī, Imām Abū Nuʿaym, *The Blessed Companions of God's Messenger*. Trans. Shaykh Muhammad al-Akili, *The Beauty of the Righteous & Ranks of the Elite*. (Philadelphia, USA, Pearl Publishing House, 1995)

Cambridge Medieval History, Vol. IV, Part I, 'The Byzantium Empire'. Ed. J. M. Hussey. (Cambridge, Cambridge Uni. Press, 1966)

———, Vol. IV, Part II, 'The Byzantium Empire – Government, Church and Civilisation'. Ed. J. M.Hussey. (Cambridge, Cambridge Uni. Press, 1967)

Cameron, Averil, *The Byzantium and Early Islamic Near East, States, resources and armies*. (Princeton, New Jersey, The Darwin Press, 1995)

Cameron, Averil and Conrad, Lawrence, *The Byzantium and Early Islamic Near East, Problems in the literary source material*. (Princeton, New Jersey, The Darwin Press, 1989)

Donner, Fred McGraw, *The Early Islamic Conquests*. (New Jersey, Princeton University Press, 1981)

Gibbon, Edward, *The History of the Decline and Fall of the Roman Empire*, Vol. III. (London, Penguin, 1995)

Hamid, Abdulwahid, *Companions of the Prophet 1*. (London, MELS, 1985)

———, *Companions of the Prophet 2*. (London, MELS, 1985)

———, *Companions of the Prophet 3*. (London, MELS, 1985)

Hamidullah, Muhammad, *The Muslim Conduct of State*. (Lahore, Sh. Muhammad Ashraf, 1942)

Hitti, Philip K., *History of the Arabs*. (London, Macmillan, 1994)

Husain, Sayed Athar, *The Glorious Khilafa*. (Lucknow, India, Academy of Islamic Research and Publications, 1980)

Kazdan, Alexandra and Constable, Giles, *People and Power in Byzantium*. (Washington, Dumbarton Oaks, 1982)

King, G. R. D. and Cameron, Averil, *The Byzantium and Early Islamic Near East, Land use and settlement pattern*. (Princeton, New Jersey, Darwin Press, 1994)

Muir, Sir William, *The Caliphate, its Rise, Decline and Fall*. (London, Darf Publishers, 1984)

Nadwi, Shaykh Abul Hasan Ali, *Islam – and the World*. International Islamic Federation of Student Organizations, 1980)

Nu'mānī, 'Allāma Shiblī, *Al-Farooq, The Life of Umar The Great Caliph of Islam*. Trans. Maulana Zafar Ali Khan. (Delhi, Immad Publications, 1987)

———, *Sīrat-un-Nabī*. Trans. M. Tayyib Bakhsh Badayuni. (Lahore, Kazi Pub., 1979)

Shahid, Irfan, *Rome and the Arabs, A Prolegomenon to the study of Byzantium and the Arabs*. (Washington, Dumbarton Oaks, 1984)

———, *Byzantium and the Arabs in the Fourth Century*. (Washington, Dumbarton Oaks, 1984)

———, *Byzantium and the Arabs in the Sixth Century*, Vols. I and II. (Washington, Dumbarton Oaks, 1995)

Shemesh, A. Ben, *Taxation in Islam*. Yaḥyā Bin Ādam's *Kitāb al-Kharāj*. (Netherlands, Leiden, E. J. Brill, 1967)

Index